PRAISE FO

"The insights i
benefit and t
—Deepak Chopra, international best-selling
author and physician

"Noah benShea is a wise and compassionate man. His writings
have touched me deeply. I highly recommend his work!"
—Jack Canfield, best-selling author of the
Chicken Soup for the Soul series

"Noah benShea is a national treasure!"
—U.S. Representative (CA) Lois Capps

"It's a very nice thing to have an old friend who is full of wit
and wisdom. For me, that friend is Noah benShea."
—Sandy Koufax, Baseball Hall of Fame

"Noah benShea is the Compass because he has, with wit,
compassion, and humor, helped so many of us to find
our way. He is like a Zen Mark Twain."
—Larry King, CNN

"Noah benShea has elevated the human spirit
to great heights with his wisdom."
—Howard Schultz, Chairman Emeritus, Starbucks

"I am proud to have Noah benShea in my life.
He is a spiritual, inspirational, and insightful man.
Everyone needs a friend like Noah."
—Herbert Simon, Chairman Emeritus, Simon Property Group,
Inc., Owner of the Indiana Pacers, and Chairman, *Kirkus Reviews*

"Noah benShea is a welcome source of
compassion and humble wisdom."
—Bob Costas, Emmy Award–winning sportscaster

"To be with Noah, to read Noah, to learn from Noah creates a deep reflection of the soul…and I am a better person to myself and those around me because of him."
—Dr. Cynthia Bioteau, President,
Florida State College at Jacksonville

"Noah's words are a spiritual roadmap to a better place."
—Gene Montesano, Founder of Lucky Brand Jeans

"Noah knows things…he is as smart as Jacob the Baker and connected to God in much the same way."
—Jeff Ayeroff, former president of A&M Records, Virgin Records, Vice Chairman Warner Bros. Music, Founder of Rock the Vote

"If you wished to create the perfect picture of an inspirational genius, you would use Noah benShea as your quintessential model."
—E. Duke Vincent, Blue Angel Aviator,
Vice Chairman of Aaron Spelling Productions

"Wise, funny, and illuminating. Noah's work is a cause for celebration." —Father Malcolm Boyd, bestselling author of *Are You Running with Me, Jesus?*

"Noah benShea's work is full of lyrical distillations of common sense, parables, aphorisms, inspirations, and truth… You might want this next to your bed for a lifetime."
—*Los Angeles Times*

"Noah's stories are not only to be read but carried in a circle around your heart…feeding you hope and humanity whenever loss of God threatens."
—Eugene Schwartz, publisher and philanthropist

"Being in the presence of Noah benShea is like coming home to your heart, where all good things happen, where we feel safe enough for introspection and expansion, where all things are possible."
—Madisyn Taylor, best-selling inspirational author; cofounder and editor-in-chief of *DailyOM*

"I was much touched and moved by Noah benShea's work."
—Dr. Jacob Neusner, National Endowment for the Humanities and National Endowment for the Arts

"Noah benShea's work is touching and charming…it is full of love of life, and of God, and of humanity."
—Rabbi Irving "Yitz" Greenberg, President, National Jewish Center for Learning and Leadership

"Noah benShea's work communicates truths… and is authored by a wise, generous spirit."
—Dr. David Lieber, former President Emeritus, University of Judaism

"Noah benShea's words are powerful and evoke a deeper meditation."
—Louis Katzoff, Editor, World Jewish Bible Society

"*We Are All Jacob's Children* is a truly beautiful book that will warm your heart and open your mind."
—Bruce Marcus, PBS Emmy-Nominated Executive Producer

WE ARE ALL
JACOB'S CHILDREN

Other books by Noah benShea include:

Jacob the Baker: Gentle Wisdom for a Complicated World

Jacob's Ladder: Wisdom for Your Heart's Ascent

Jacob's Journey: Wisdom to Find Your Way; Strength to Carry On

The Word: Jewish Wisdom Through Time

Great Quotes to Inspire Great Teachers

A Compass for Teaching

A Compass for Healing

Great Recovery Quotes and Stories to Inspire Great Healers

Great Recovery Quotes and Stories to Inspire Great Healing

The Journey to Greatness: National Public Television Edition (PBS Series)

WE ARE ALL JACOB'S CHILDREN

A TALE OF HOPE, WISDOM, AND FAITH

NOAH BEN SHEA

Copyright © 2018 Noah benShea
All rights reserved. This book or any portion thereof
may not be reproduced or used in any manner whatsoever
without the express written permission of the publisher
except for the use of brief quotations in a book review.

Printed in the United States of America

First Edition

Cover illustration by Michael Marsicano

Thank you, Herbert Simon.
Thank you, Carissa Bluestone.
Thank you, Lauren Bailey.
Thank you, Michael, Alex, and Jillian.
Thank you, for you.

ISBN 978-1-7324760-0-4

www.noahbenshea.com

To those who came before me.
To those who will come after.
To those I love.
And have loved me.
La vita è breve!
Reality is only a memory ahead of its time.

In memory of Fabiola Benitez

Welcome Eli Saticoy benShea

Family is a way of holding hands with forever.

CONTENTS

Preface 3

    Wake Me 5

PART I: WE ARE TOURISTS IN THE NOW 7

    We are tourists in the now.. 9

    In life, we can feel profoundly blessed
and profoundly sad at the same time.. 10

    Put your faith—not your fears—in charge.. 11

    When life calls the roll, answer, "Present." 13

    Caring can be the right answer
to almost any question.. 14

    Listening is the best way
to begin a conversation.. 17

    Love without honesty is betrayal.
Honesty without love is cruelty.. 19

PART II: FAITH AND REASON 21

    You are special...just like everyone else. 23

    Too humble is half-proud. 24

    There is no success, only practice. 25

    Everything is pending. 26

    Only God can decide when it's time to open a rose. . . . 27

    Sometimes just feeling okay is okay. 28

    We all remember what we want to forget. 29

    The reason for faith is not reason. 30

We don't need faith to find gold.
We need faith for when we don't find it. 31

God is family to people of faith. 33

PART III: THE HERE AND NOW IS NOW AND HERE . . 35

Life is a time machine. 37

You better like your strengths,
because you'll pay for them. 39

To be called in life
doesn't necessarily make it our calling. 41

The world changes when we do. 43

Don't react—respond. 44

Attitude is altitude. 46

To know you are blessed is its own blessing. 48

Making someone else happy is not your work. 49

Love is kindness regardless of the weather. 52

When you see the wind,
you are watching God breathe. 54

Little makes us better company to others
than being good company to ourselves. 56

The here and now is now and here. 58

Our dreams are poets who wait until we fall asleep
to find their voice. 61

PART IV: A LEAP OF FAITH 65

Anyone can be right.
Wisdom is what we learn from being wrong. 67

You're not young enough to know everything. 69

If we learn to laugh at ourselves,
our lives will never be without amusement. 71

Luck is a strange cane.
It only serves us when we don't lean on it. 72

Memory is the secret garden.. 74

Even secret gardens need water.. 75

When the student is ready,
the teacher will appear—and vice versa. 77

The cost for any of us at any moment
is always the cost of who we are
against the cost of who we might yet be.. 79

The easy path is not always the easy way. 81

We are all alone.
But we are all alone together.. 83

To hear the truth,
we only have to listen for our deafness. 85

If you argue with a fool,
there are two fools talking.. 87

To live long, live slowly. 88

PART V: HOPE IS ITS OWN REALITY **89**

Not everyone who is crying is crying out loud. 91

Parents have as much responsibility
to be students as they do teachers.. 93

Fear is where courage is born.. 95

Even a broken clock is right twice a day.. 96

In each of us there is a better person
we too often confuse with someone else. 97

It's not what you're thinking,
but how you're thinking it.. 99

Killing time is the worst form of littering. 100

Change is the way the river runs.
Progress is when we change the way we run. 101

Be self-accountable, not self-abusive.. 102

Over every finish line in life are the words, "Begin here!". . 104

In each of us there is a place where
we are better than our fears. 105

No one can take your good deeds,
and no one tries to steal your troubles. 106

PART VI: FINDING THE DOOR 109

Prayer is a path where there is none. 111

It is a wonder to grow old
if we grant our wonder
the right to be born again. 112

Our grasp is only exceeded by
what can slip between our fingers. 113

Hope is a friend we can all turn to. 115

Those who live on the edge, grow wings. 116

Don't let the past kidnap your future.. 118

Sadness and joy can fly—away. 121

PART VII: WE ARE ALL JACOB'S CHILDREN 123

Wisdom is where we are wise enough to find it. 125

Tears falling on our cheeks can cause us to bloom. 127

Of all the things you can make in life,
why not make a difference? 129

You are the paint, the painter, and the painting. 131

In "Once upon a time," God is time. 133

Honesty is the door to all wisdom;
humility is the door to all honesty. 135

All private deceit eventually becomes public deceit. 136

Honest confusion can be honest prayer. 138

Our soul does not bear the burden of our body. 140

The absent bird does not leave us absent of its song. . . .142

The work in life isn't what you do but who you are.. 143

God is never so with us as when we feel alone. 145

No one has ever found their way
who has not felt lost.. 146

An army of sheep led by a lion will defeat
an army of lions led by a sheep. 148

You don't have to die to be reincarnated. 150

A great fisherman is someone who catches himself
just in time.. 151

The people we love and lose are not lost. 153

Be more. Want less. Care more. Take less. 154

Inside every parent is a child needing to be loved. 156

It is the silence between the notes
that makes the music. 159

Knowing doesn't change the weather.. 162

In peace, find gratitude.. 163

People seek emotional help
when they are feeling too much
or when they are not feeling at all. 164

God put one hand in another and felt the hearts fit. 167

Anyone can count the number of seeds in an apple.
No one can count the number of apples in a seed. 169

People of all faiths are of one faith
if their religion is kindness. 172

We're not expected to finish our work,
but neither are we excused from it.. 176

Forever may not be long enough. 178

About the Author 181

Dear Reader,

When *Jacob the Baker* was first published, I was repeatedly asked if Jacob and I were the same person. And I faithfully answered, "Yes, but I'm the one with character flaws."

Jacob and I have now been together for over forty years, and I think that admission still holds.

The Jacob the Baker books have been both national and international best sellers. They have been translated into eighteen languages and are embraced by millions around the world.

If you have not read the earlier Jacob the Baker books, please accept this invitation. And yet, do not hesitate to begin here, because as Jacob would remind us, *"In life, that you begin is often more important than where you begin."*

Thank you for your patience in waiting for this effort to be born. It has taken me a lifetime, guided and lifted me in many ways, and reminded me of the work still on my path. Surely, this book would not have been possible without the embrace of Grace. Apparently, God isn't done with me yet. Or you, I trust.

I am blessed to have this work and pass this blessing into your hands. May you, dear reader, go from strength to strength, and be a source of strength to others.

Amen.

Noah

*Jacob is wholehearted and wise.
He is an anonymous soul
who has lived without notice
in every century,
in every corner of the world,
even as the world passes
in its habit of hurry and inattention.
Until…*

Preface

Life is lived forwards but understood backwards.

—Kierkegaard

Jacob the Baker is the tale of a poor but pious baker who lives an anonymous life in a timeless world.

While waiting for the ovens to come to temperature in the predawn morning, Jacob would write notes to himself, trying to make sense of life.

One morning, one of his notes accidentally fell into the dough and was baked into a loaf of bread.

The woman who bought the bread came upon the message and was profoundly moved by its compassion and wisdom. She rushed to the bakery to see who wrote the note.

There she discovered Jacob the Baker, and soon the whole town, and then the wider world, realized someone special was living among them.

From far and wide people traveled to the bakery just to ask Jacob questions and listen to his parables about life, prayer, and love.

The community's children came to the bakery after school to sit on the flour sacks and hear his wisdom and stories.

If those around him were asked to describe Jacob's message, they would touch their hearts and answer, "Jacob the Baker offers gentle wisdom for a complicated world." And if asked where Jacob lived, they would smile and answer, "At the intersection of hope, comfort, and direction!"

WAKE ME

*And when the voice came,
Jacob heard it not from a place far away
but from a place deep within.*

*Dreaming hope against reality;
knowing hope was its own reality,
here was an awakening even as Jacob was not awake.*

*Do not come to tell me of the long sleep ahead.
Come instead to wake me
And make me see the moon.*

*Do not come to tell me the hour's growing late.
Come instead to shake me
And remind me light is on the lake.*

*Do not come to tell me I must be cautious in my ways.
Come instead to promise that if I live a life that's bold
What grows will not grow old.*

*Do not come to tell me this life's a slender thread.
Come instead to compass me
That there is a road ahead.*

*Do not come to tell me of the worries I should fear.
Come instead to sing to me
Songs of faith I wait to hear.*

Do not come to tell me memories of who is gone.
Come instead to tell me that
All passes, but nothing's gone.

Do not come to tell me life is sad.
Come instead to laugh with me
And offer oath
That health alone is reason to be glad.

Do not come to tell me of the long sleep ahead.
Come instead to wake me.
Come instead to teach me.
Come instead so I will know
The here and now is now and here,
And those are blessed
Who in your Grace
Make rest
From their fear.

Part I

We Are Tourists in the Now

WE ARE TOURISTS IN THE NOW.

———

It was the last turn of dark before the dawn—the crack between the worlds.

The morning light hinted at its intentions without giving up its secrets.

Jacob folded the pillow in half and propped it behind his neck so he might look out the window.

He watched the shadow world of green leaves wave slowly back and forth as if in a syncopated meditation like that of a metronome.

In this moment, Jacob observed the day without the bias of expectation. He let judgment have its rest and was certain only of life's uncertainty.

The road ahead is the path within, thought Jacob.

Then he opened his heart, released his mind, and entered prayer.

Here was pause without borders.

Here was the Grace of faith.

Here, he knew, was his soul's safe place.

And the chorus of silence said, "Amen."

Jacob rolled from his side of the bed and placed both feet on the floor. He sat there wordless, motionless, watching his feet.

I am a tourist in the now.

In life, we can feel profoundly blessed and profoundly sad at the same time.

Rising slowly, Jacob stood and looked over his shoulder.

The opposite side of his bed lay undisturbed, perfectly made. He had not slept on that side of the bed since Ruth had passed.

In the bed's neatness, he saw both her absence and her presence.

Before Jacob fell asleep, he would lean across the pillows and kiss Ruth good night. And she would kiss him back, across time, across the cool cotton of the pillows.

He did not seek to understand why he had this habit. The experience of the habit trumped his understanding.

While Jacob had always been inclined to speak his mind, he was more inclined to speak from his heart.

And even as Ruth was given leave of her mortal body, Jacob would not leave her. His heart had staked its ground.

If some voice argued that this was romantic but unrealistic, Jacob held tight to the romantic.

If those quoting Scripture would remind Jacob to "choose life," Jacob would affirm, *This is how I choose to live.*

Ruth once said, "My lover, you are wise, but knowledge is not always a soft bed, and wisdom is not to be confused with a comforter."

Now Jacob looked at Ruth's side of the bed and again thought about what he wished he did not know.

And the wheel was spinning.

And the day dawned with implications yet unborn.

Put your faith—not your fears—in charge.

For years, it was Jacob's morning ritual to enjoy a crust of rustic bread brushed with honey and a cup of hot tea. This ritual was its own nourishment.

And before breaking bread he said a prayer that nourished his spirit and mended his soul.

Each truth was a key to the truth that followed.

Each truth was wrapped parenthetically in a breath and exhalation.

"In gratitude," said Jacob, "find prayer.

"In prayer, find faith.

"In faith, find Grace.

"In Grace, find peace.

"In peace, find gratitude."

Centered, filled with the peace of gratitude, Jacob exhaled slowly.

Here was a man watching the stirrings in his own cocoon from the outside.

The moment held like sound waves from a copper bell—though the inattentive would think that the bell had long stopped ringing.

Then, from somewhere beyond the borders of what passed as reality's voice, Ruth spoke to Jacob.

"Jacob, do not weep at what has passed; smile that it passed our way."

Jacob was silent.

"Jacob," said Ruth, her voice its own embrace, "be a source of strength to others. That is why you are here."

For Jacob, that Ruth had left did not mean she was gone. And so,

Jacob replied to Ruth, he knew he was in an empty room and yet not alone.

"My dear," said Jacob, "what if I no longer want to answer questions for which I also have questions?"

Now it was Ruth's turn to be silent.

But in her absence, two angels circled above Jacob's home. They had orders to watch over this man.

And their calling to be his guardians honored Jacob's choice to be a man not without doubts but one who put his faith, and not his fears, in charge.

When life calls the roll, answer, "Present."

In Jacob's world, time did not march to humanity's rush.

If Jacob had been asked to explain how this was possible, he would have answered, "An eternity is any moment of patience."

If asked to explain patience, he would have answered with one of Ruth's favorite sayings: "Patience is a cathedral of opportunity."

Once, a man pursuing his own turmoil had asked Jacob, "What do I need to do now?"

Jacob simply answered, "Be present."

Now, in the present, Jacob heard a tapping at his front door—and a child's voice.

"Jacob? Jacob, may we ask you a question?"

Jacob opened the door and saw a little boy holding hands with a little girl. The two of them stood very still, held in the moment and by the moment.

When the children saw they had Jacob's focus, they said in nervous unison, "Please."

Jacob took a long breath, watching his own uncertainty in the mix of events that had all taken place so quickly that morning—and on several planes of reality. With this inhalation, he shifted his attention from the children to the bedroom.

His eyes came to rest on Ruth's pillow.

The boy turned to the girl and asked, "What's he doing? Do you think he knows we're here?"

Jacob turned to the children and said, "He knows."

Caring can be the right answer to almost any question.

———

It was as if the light from the windows streamed in synchronicity with the glow of the children's faces.

"You didn't expect us, did you?" asked the girl.

"Life can be an unexpected joy," said Jacob. "I choose to expect that."

The children giggled.

With the exaggerated motion of a maître d', Jacob invited the children to come into his home and sit at the table where he took his morning tea.

He left the door open behind them. They noticed. He noticed that they noticed.

The children's legs dangled over the edge of the chairs. Their eyes danced around the room, clearly taking in the details.

In a voice suggesting nothing was out of the ordinary, Jacob asked, "Would you like something to eat?"

The boy looked at the girl. The girl looked at the boy. Then she lifted her chin as if urging the boy to begin.

"Don't you want to know who we are?" asked the boy.

"I want to know if you are hungry," said Jacob.

"That isn't the question my brother asked you," said the girl.

"Caring can be the right answer to almost any question," said Jacob. "Would you like some soup?"

The move from ideas to soup threw the children for a moment, then they understood.

"Yes, please," said the girl, clearly the younger of the two but already born to be the older. "And my brother would like some too."

"Okay," said Jacob, "first soup, and then questions."

"And crackers," said the girl.

"Yes, of course," said Jacob, "crackers." He went over to the stove to warm the soup.

When Jacob returned to the table, the girl smashed the crackers with her tiny fist.

Her brother jumped at the sound and gave her a look. And she gave it back to him. When he slurped his soup, she gave him the same look again.

"Jacob," said the girl, after tasting her first spoonful, "I like your soup. And I think we like you. But we don't really know you."

"Ah," said Jacob, and he laughed. "Aren't all our friends strangers when we meet them?"

The children thought about that for a moment, and then the boy asked, "Do you like being smart?"

"I've never asked myself that question," said Jacob. "I like to think there are many things more interesting to ponder than if you think you're smart."

The little girl pursed her lips. "What if I think you're kind of smart?"

Jacob laughed. "I half agree. I think you're kind."

"And you think that's important?" asked the little girl.

"What's important," said Jacob, "is remembering that everyone's important."

"That's pretty smart," said the girl.

"Well," said Jacob, "a *very* smart man once said, 'The three most important rules in life are: Be kind, be kind, be kind.'"

"Whew," said the little girl to her brother. "I told you we came to the right place."

"She always thinks she's right," said the boy.

Jacob laughed. "Too many of us worry more about being right than doing right."

The little girl thought on that, then nodded and offered Jacob both her bowl and her smile. "May I have a little more? I'm beginning to get warm."

"Yes," said Jacob, cradling the smile for safekeeping. He too felt warm, maybe for the first time in a long time.

Listening is the best way to begin a conversation.

———

"Go ahead," said the little girl to her brother. "Ask him."

"Okay, okay," said the boy, buttoning up his courage. "Everybody in the village says that if you have a problem or a question, go see Jacob the Baker. But they also say you don't go to the bakery much anymore." The boy paused to catch his breath and to read any reaction from Jacob.

"And," said the girl, "we know we're children, but we have a problem."

"Well," said Jacob, "little people can have big problems, and big people often make little problems into something much bigger."

"Too big," said the girl, opening her arms to show how big.

"But before we solve problems, may I learn your names?" asked Jacob.

"See," said the little girl, now chiding Jacob, "I told you, you should have listened to my brother and asked us who we are when we got here!"

"You're right," said Jacob. "I apologize. Listening is the best way to begin a conversation."

"Don't worry about her," said the boy. "She always tells people what to do."

"Worry's work is to arrive at worry," said Jacob, reminding himself as much as responding.

The little girl listened, cocked her head in thought, and said, "Yep, you're smart. I'm Sophie, and he's Caleb." She smiled again but then gestured as if attempting to move things along. "Let's get to our problem."

Jacob was entranced by the child's directness.

"Our problem," said Sophie, "is that our parents are acting like they don't know who they are."

"Ahh," said Jacob.

"What does 'Ahh' mean?" asked Caleb.

"It means I am thinking," said Jacob.

"Come on, what are you thinking?"

"I'm thinking about how easy it is for any of us to forget what we don't want to remember. Or to lose our way when we decide to forget why we lost our way before."

"Then our parents have definitely lost their way…" said Sophie. "And we want you to tell us what to do."

"What do you think you should do?" asked Jacob.

"We don't know. We're kids," said Caleb.

"Sort of," said Sophie.

Jacob laughed, and while he was conscious of his growing ease in the company of these children, he also thought he should be cautious of being too intrusive.

The children sat there while Jacob debated with himself.

"You're taking a long time," said Sophie.

"Time takes all of us," said Jacob.

"Is that why you don't wear a watch?" asked Caleb.

"Time doesn't wear a watch," said Jacob.

"Do you learn that when you're old?" asked Sophie.

"You learn it," said Jacob, "whenever you take the time to learn it."

"And is it different for kids?" asked Sophie.

"Sort of," said Jacob. "The young worry that the future will never come; the old worry that it will."

Love without honesty is betrayal. Honesty without love is cruelty.

———

"Jacob," said Sophie, "we really want your advice. What do you think we should say to our parents?"

"Be loving and speak the truth," said Jacob. "What other people hear is their work."

"Even parents?" asked Caleb.

"Even parents," said Jacob.

"Because?" asked Sophie.

"Because," said Jacob, "love without honesty is betrayal, and honesty without love is cruelty."

"That's a lot for kids to remember," said Caleb.

"That's a lot for any of us to remember," said Jacob. "Whether we're grown-ups or growing up, we often don't tell others the truth because we're afraid they'll get angry, or think less of us, or won't like us."

"So?" said the boy.

"So," said Jacob, "too often it's not until we get angry that we tell someone the truth."

"And then?"

"And then," said Jacob, "the people we're talking to get angry back, and everyone in the conversation gets lost in the anger. So, no one finds their way to the truth."

Jacob stopped, looked at the children, and wondered if he needed to back up and try that again.

But that wasn't necessary, at least not for Sophie.

"So that means," said Sophie, smoothing the sides of her small dress, "if we're honest and loving with someone, and they get angry with us, we should tell them we can't accept their anger because taking something that isn't ours is not honest."

Jacob just stared at her.

"Okay, now what are you thinking?" she asked.

"I'm thinking I should be coming to you for advice," replied Jacob.

"Oh, you will," said Sophie. "Be patient."

While Jacob thought on that, Caleb jumped in. "Jacob, thank you for not talking to us like we're children who don't know anything."

"And thank you," said Jacob, "for not confusing me with an adult who thinks he knows everything."

Part II

―◆―

Faith and Reason

You are special...just like everyone else.

After the children left, Jacob couldn't dismiss the timing of their visit—arriving on the same morning's tide as Ruth's reminder.

Staring at the empty soup bowls, Jacob remembered a great teacher once saying, "Coincidence is God's way of remaining anonymous."

And coincidence was still at play.

When Jacob stepped out into the morning, he found himself surrounded by a circle of waiting clerics.

"Jacob," said the leader, "we have long heard of you and have traveled a great distance with our questions."

The others simply took this explanation as their invitation to begin.

"Jacob, do you think God knows who we are when we pray?"

"Knowing who we are isn't God's work," said Jacob. "It is our work."

"What if we don't think we're anyone special?"

"Oh, you are special," said Jacob.

"We are?"

"Yes," said Jacob, "just like everyone else."

Too humble is half-proud.

With a determined politeness, the queries continued around the circle.
"Jacob, tell me what I should know about praying."
"Don't confuse knowing with praying," said Jacob.
"But I'm an important man; people expect me to know these things."
"Don't confuse being important with self-importance," said Jacob.
"So I can't take pride in how I pray?"
"Pride," said Jacob, "is a slippery slope."
"How slippery?"
"Well," said Jacob, "once there was a man whose spiritual community voted him the most humble and gave him a medal. The next week, when he came to pray, he wore the medal, and they took it away from him."
"What am I to learn from this?" asked the man.
"Too humble," said Jacob, "is half-proud."

There is no success, only practice.

"Jacob," asked another of the clerics hesitantly, "what do you think is the right attitude to prepare one for what the day-to-day can bring?"

"Prepare but do not presume," said Jacob.

"What is the difference?"

"We have to walk down life's path," said Jacob, "prepared for the greatest joy to leap out and embrace us at any moment.

"And we have to walk down life's path prepared for the greatest evil to leap out and attack us at any moment.

"And we have to walk down life's path prepared for absolutely nothing to happen at any moment.

"And we have to walk down life's path prepared for any and none of these things to happen concurrently."

The cleric was stunned. "Who can live this way?"

"You can, brother," said Jacob.

"What if I fail?"

"We all do," said Jacob. "That's why I called you brother."

"Well, what if I succeed?"

"There is no success," said Jacob, "only practice."

Everything is pending.

―

Now, in the synchronicity of both questions and answers, a concerned voice tugged for Jacob's attention.

"Jacob, I am not a religious man, but of course I would also like to know what lies ahead in my life."

"Everything lies ahead," said Jacob.

"Why is that?"

"Because everything is pending," said Jacob.

"But," said the worried voice, "there must be something I can count on?"

"There is," said Jacob. "Everything is pending."

"But what about my fear of missing something in my life?"

"My friend," said Jacob, "often the only thing missing in our life is us."

Only God can decide when it's time to open a rose.

———

A woman who had been waiting outside the circle of clerics spoke hesitantly, almost intimately. "Jacob, do you think God knows what we are really thinking?"

"Only God knows God's mind," said Jacob.

"But I worry sometimes," said the woman, "about the things I'm thinking…"

"We're better served," said Jacob, "to worry less about what we're thinking and more about why we're not thinking."

"What about when things aren't going the way I want?"

"God is not a cosmic gardener here to do your weeding," said Jacob. "When you can't change events, change you."

"And if I fail?"

"God weeps for those who cry," said Jacob, "but not for those who don't try."

The woman thought about that for a moment, and then said, "So life's garden blooms on God's timetable."

"You'll have to ask the Gardener," said Jacob.

"But what do you think?"

"I think," said Jacob, "only God can decide when it's time to open a rose."

Sometimes just feeling okay is okay.

―

Jacob saw that the clerics had attracted a growing group of onlookers. Now a confessional voice broke in from the crowd. "Jacob, I wish praying made me feel better."

"Prayer isn't supposed to make you feel better—only *be* better," said Jacob.

"And that's okay?"

"Sometimes," said Jacob, "just feeling okay is okay."

"And if we pray and hear nothing, do you think God is listening?"

"Ask God," said Jacob.

"You're not listening to me," said the man.

"I didn't think your question was whether I was the one listening," said Jacob.

We all remember what we want to forget.

―――

A young man was wide-eyed as he listened to the questions posed to Jacob and the insight in his replies.

"Jacob," asked the man, "how do you remember all the things you say?"

"I don't," said Jacob.

"I don't understand."

"If you remember who you are," said Jacob, letting his eyes lock on the questioner, "you don't have to remember your lines."

"Is that true for all of us?"

"In any of us are all of us," said Jacob.

"That's hard to comprehend," said the young man.

"For any of us," said Jacob.

The reason for faith is not reason.

———

Another bystander cleared his throat. "Jacob, I am a man of science who wants to know what you think is the reason for faith."

"The reason for faith is not reason," said Jacob.

"Then why pray?"

"Life is a gift," said Jacob. "Prayer is a thank-you note."

"And?"

Now Jacob laughed. "And didn't your mother tell you to send your thank-you notes?"

"That's it?" asked the man. "That's why you pray?"

"No," said Jacob, smiling. "It's simpler than that. If we don't pray, we don't have a prayer."

"What if I pray but get no reply?" asked the man, exasperated.

"Faith premised on response is not faith," said Jacob.

"I can't see how this makes sense," said the man.

"Of course, you are right," said Jacob.

"I am?"

"Yes," said Jacob, "faith is a witness to things unseen."

WE DON'T NEED FAITH TO FIND GOLD. WE NEED FAITH FOR WHEN WE DON'T FIND IT.

———

A man older and more senior stepped closer. His voice was tinged with anguish.

"Jacob, how can a person find their integrity?"

"The portal to integrity is honesty," said Jacob.

"I don't understand."

"Integrity," said Jacob, "is when you tell yourself the truth. Honesty is when you tell someone else the truth."

"But to do this," said the man, "takes faith—isn't faith difficult for people to find?"

"You are right," said Jacob. "Too many of us live with our eyes wide open shut."

"Huh?"

"Too many of us," said Jacob, "are self-blinding for fear of what we'll see."

"So we're afraid to open our eyes?"

"Or we forget," said Jacob, "that when we shut our eyes, God does not go into hiding."

"But what about those of us who hold God on high?" asked the man.

"Sometimes on high is too high," said Jacob.

"I don't mean to sound childish, but how high is too high?"

"Too high," said Jacob, "is when we elevate God to irrelevance by placing God on a shelf too high to reach."

"So to reach God…"

"You have to reach inside you."

"Even when it's difficult?"

"We don't need faith to find gold," said Jacob. "We need faith for when we don't find it."

God is family to people of faith.

"Jacob," shouted a woman at the back of the crowd, "what if others disappoint me? What if others let me down?"

"Then perhaps you will despair," said Jacob softly, "but if you're not disappointed by how you conduct yourself, you won't be disappointed in you."

"So, that's it? How I conduct myself is all I can examine?"

"That is enough for most of us to do."

"So faith begins with me."

"In you."

"And to look for God…?"

"Look out for others."

"Like we're all a family?"

"Yes."

"Because?"

"Because God is family to people of faith," said Jacob.

"And if we are not of that faith?"

"Those who don't make the world a kinder place will make it sadder."

"Are you sure?"

"Sadly, I am," said Jacob.

Part III

———

*The Here and Now
Is Now and Here*

Life is a time machine.

―

The spin was on. Time turned and turned again. Day became night; night became another day.

In a habit worn familiar by time, Jacob lifted his coat from the hook and once again began his journey to the bakery before dawn.

Over his shoulder was a sliver of crescent moon.

Beneath his feet was the sound of the snow's crust breaking under his boots.

Jacob remembered the quiet invite he once treasured in arriving at the bakery before the others would reach for their aprons.

He remembered feeling like a boy again when he could warm his winter cheek by the ovens.

He remembered the grace of solitude in being alone in the bakery and writing notes to himself in an attempt to make sense of life.

He remembered his life before the world found his notes in their bread, whispered their discoveries into shouts, and sought his answers to their questions.

He remembered the children's smiles while they sat on the flour sacks and listened to his stories.

And even as these memories were his company, Jacob was also reunited for a moment with Ruth and with Jonah, an orphan who had lived as a son to Jacob and Ruth and grown up to become the Elder of a council of sages in a distant community.

And both of those whom had come into his life, now were absent.

And standing there alone, he thought of all the leaving inherent in everything that arrives.

Life is a time machine, thought Jacob. *We can go backward in our memories.*

We can go forward in our vision. But the helm is only in the now.
And there is a Hand larger than ours on the helm.

You better like your strengths, because you'll pay for them.

In a well-practiced ritual, Jacob took the crumbs he saved from his morning bread and tossed them to the pigeons from the bakery's back door.

The birds rose in pandemonium, the sound of their wings mimicking applause.

It was as if one generation of pigeons had counseled those who came after them on the pending reward of Jacob's return.

When Jacob stepped into the bakery, he was reunited with a comfort long missed but not forgotten.

Before the door behind even closed, Jacob could hear the slapping sound of bread pans being stacked and falling to fit on top of one another.

And most familiar was the cloud of flour dust moving toward him.

Inside the cloud, Jacob saw his old friend Samuel, the owner of the bakery.

"Oh, oh, oh," shouted Samuel, "friendship returns with a friend's face."

Jacob stepped closer and brushed the flour dust from Samuel's hair.

"Not so fast with the brushing," said Samuel. "I remember when you still took honor from the flour dust in your hair."

"And I give you honor," said Jacob, tossing a handful of flour into the air as if he were an ancient messenger greeting a monarch.

Jacob loved Samuel. Samuel loved Jacob. In this, there was no complication.

Their bond across time was shaped by respect and filled with laughter.

"Let's take a look at you," said Samuel, stepping back to take measure. "Ah yes, the same twinkle in your eye, maybe a little white in your beard. But I still see strength."

"My friend," said Jacob, "strength isn't measured in the absence of weakness but in how well we wrestle with our weaknesses."

"You see," said Samuel, "clearly you are still Jacob the Baker, and the little you ever forget is more than I will ever learn."

Jacob didn't say anything.

"And," said Samuel, "of course you are still uncomfortable with my mentioning your gifts."

Jacob laughed. "I remember my grandfather once cautioned a powerful man: 'You better like your strengths because you'll pay for them.'"

"Should I take notes?" asked Samuel, pretending he was scribbling.

Jacob laughed again. "No need. The truth is no less true when it is ignored. And no more true when it is agreed upon."

TO BE CALLED IN LIFE
DOESN'T NECESSARILY MAKE IT OUR CALLING.

———

Jacob took a baker's cotton apron from the pile on the proofing bench.

"Okay," said Jacob to Samuel, "shall we get this bakery to open its eyes?"

"Of course," said Samuel, "but just to be clear…Aren't you the one who told me that to make a friend, sometimes you have to shut one eye, and to keep a friend, sometimes you have to shut two eyes?"

"Yes," said Jacob, looking over his shoulder as he began to fire the ovens. "And sadly, too many have lived in the dark for so long they are blinded when they come into the light."

"Aren't we all in the dark?" asked Samuel.

"The Eternal Light is an internal light," said Jacob.

Samuel shut his eyes and nodded resolutely.

When Jacob and Samuel worked together, it wasn't work. When they finished, and the loaves were set to rest and rise, Samuel put his arm around Jacob's shoulder and said, "Have you heard what the world is singing about your son, Jonah?"

Jacob smiled. "People still call him my son?"

Samuel shrugged. "Aren't you the one who said, 'The truth is seldom hidden but often overlooked'?"

Jacob said nothing.

"Of course Jonah says he's your son," said Samuel. "Jonah is a truth teller raised by a truth teller. He makes it very clear to the world that he was an orphan whom you took into your home, and your heart, and your wisdom. When others speak of his caring, Jonah says it was Jacob who fathered in him a passion for compassion."

Samuel was now picking up Samuel speed. "And when others praise him—as they should, because he is the youngest ever to be the Elder of the Sages—Jonah says, 'You should meet Jacob the Baker.'

"And," said Samuel, rubbing his chin in thought, "if I remember correctly, many years ago, you were called upon to be the Elder."

"Yes."

"And why didn't you accept?"

"To be called in life doesn't necessarily make it our calling."

"Okay, so what calls you now?"

"Right now, I don't know," said Jacob with an air of the confession.

"Shhh," said Samuel mockingly. "If people heard Jacob the Baker speaking this way, they would think you are human."

Jacob again waved off the exaggeration and said, "My friend, all honesty begins with self-honesty."

"And those who lie to themselves?" asked Samuel.

"Will eventually lie to the world," said Jacob.

"So tell me the truth," said Samuel. "Are you here this morning just as a visitor?"

"Do you know anyone who isn't a visitor?" asked Jacob, motioning to the world around them.

First Samuel laughed, and then he tapped his chest and said, "Jacob, I'll tell you what you taught this visitor when I was a younger man. You said, 'Samuel, the best way to get where you are going is to be where you are. Reality is only a memory ahead of its time.'"

"And you still remember that?" asked Jacob.

"I remember it like it was yesterday," said Samuel, imitating Jacob in waving off a compliment. "Only I can't remember what happened yesterday."

The world changes when we do.

―

"You know, Jacob," said Samuel, studying his friend's face, "you've changed."

"Well," said Jacob, "change is the only constant."

"Aha," said Samuel. "I do remember the first time you said that."

"Then you also remember that memory is the gentlest of truths," said Jacob.

"Okay, okay," said Samuel. "I may not be old yet, but I know I am in the waiting room. So, instead of remembering, can you teach me about forgetting?"

"Forgetting can be a blessing," said Jacob, "even as what we remember can be a stone in our shoe."

"Then I am truly blessed," said Samuel, laughing.

"But," said Jacob, "a great sage has taught us that forgiving can be even more blessed than forgetting."

"Why?"

"Because it is forgiving in spite of remembering."

"And what would you advise me, your friend Samuel, never to forget?"

"The world changes when we do," said Jacob.

And even as he answered this question, Jacob knew he was talking to himself.

Don't react—respond.

"Jacob," said Samuel, "I know many people still stop you with their questions, so certainly you are aware that you continue to play an important part in a lot of lives."

"No matter what part we play in life," said Jacob, "it is important to play the part and not the result."

"Aha," said Samuel. "And do you think most of us fail to do this because we don't know this?"

"No," said Jacob. "Most of us don't lack for information. What most of us lack is the character to act on the information at hand."

"So when we fail ourselves, it's not a matter of being right or wrong?"

"That is a distraction," said Jacob. "Being right doesn't make you righteous."

"And the self-righteous?"

"Anyone looking down on others," said Jacob, "is not looking up at God."

Even as Jacob answered his questions, Samuel could see his friend was deep in thought.

"Tell me what you are thinking. Talk to me," said Samuel.

When Jacob replied, the rhythm in what he said was like a man stepping slowly from rock to rock in an effort to cross a dark stream.

"The number one illness among all people is depression.

"The number one reason for depression is stress.

"And the number one cause of stress is people trying to control what they cannot control."

"The lesson?" asked Samuel, his eyes locked on Jacob's.

"We are not in charge of what the world delivers to our door," said Jacob. "We are in charge of our response."

"And the challenge?"

"The challenge," said Jacob, "is to respond—not react."

Attitude is altitude.

This conversation between friends was a long time coming. Both had witnessed life's impact on the other as well as on themselves.

"Jacob," said Samuel, "many years ago you gave me pause when I heard you say, 'Life is sometimes heavy only because we attempt to carry it.' And yet, even today, so many, many people feel they are under very heavy stress."

"The weight of stress," said Jacob, "is in many ways the weight we give it."

"I don't understand," said Samuel.

"Imagine stress is a glass of water," said Jacob. "To lift the glass is not a burden. But the longer we are required to hold the glass up, the heavier it becomes. The glass's weight after five minutes would be bearable. But to hold it up for five hours or five years would be torture."

"So?"

"So," said Jacob, "stress's weight, and its burden in our lives, is dramatically influenced by how long we hold on to our stress."

"Therefore, for the stress in our life to weigh less, we have to…?"

"Let go of our commitment to hold on to our stress," said Jacob.

"And lift our spirits instead?"

"And to lift our spirits, we often only have to stop doing what is bringing us down. Attitude is altitude."

"But," said Samuel, "some people think stress gives them energy."

Jacob laughed. "Some people think that setting their pants on fire is a good way to get warm."

"But what about those people who say they are just used to feeling stressed?" asked Samuel.

"If you lie down in warm water for long enough," said Jacob, "you won't know when you're cooked."

To know you are blessed is its own blessing.

Samuel stood there, looking at his friend and weighing the moment.

Then, slowly but with conviction, Samuel said, "Listen to me, Jacob. You are a blessing. And whether you are Jacob the Baker or not, you are Jacob, and you remain a teacher. Even if you're still learning this."

Jacob could hear Ruth in his ear, "Are you listening?"

"What do you think Ruth would say?" asked Samuel.

Jacob laughed. "I think she would say, 'When school is out, school is not out.'"

"So, teacher," Samuel said, "have you made up your mind about what you're going to do now?"

"A great teacher," said Jacob, "reminded us: 'All of our final decisions are made in states of mind that do not last.'"

"But you're okay with the changes that are at your door?" asked Samuel.

"Change," said Jacob, "is not a revolving door but an evolving door."

"And?"

"And change doesn't always knock at our door; sometimes it simply kicks it down."

"Just so we're clear on this," said Samuel, "in my mind you're a blessing."

"And in my mind," said Jacob, "to know you are blessed is its own blessing."

Making someone else happy is not your work.

As Jacob left the bakery that afternoon, he was surprised to see a middle-aged couple standing in the cold with their backs to each other. They were stamping their feet to stay warm.

"Ah, Jacob, finally," said the man. "We were hoping to speak with you when no one else was around."

"Well," said Jacob, looking up at the few pigeons still on the rain gutters, "I think you are successful."

"Good," said the woman. "We very badly want to ask your opinion about some things that are not good in our relationship."

"Sometimes what we want badly serves us badly," said Jacob.

The woman looked confused, and Jacob wanted to be helpful, but he was also feeling a little trapped by the circumstances. "Look, I'm just a man who used to be a baker, and now—"

"We know who you are," said the man, "and we know you are wise."

"Nobody's perfect," said Jacob, turning sideways to the compliment.

"Oh, Jacob," said the man, "we just want to ask you a couple of questions." Before Jacob could respond, the man continued. "For as long as we've been married, my wife has always told me what to do. And I don't like being bossed around. What should I say to her?"

"Say thank you," said Jacob.

"Say thank you?"

"Yes, thank her for her opinion," said Jacob. "And do what you want to do."

The man looked puzzled.

"It's not confusing," said Jacob. "Don't do what she wants you to do and then blame her for controlling you."

"But she *is* controlling me."

"No," said Jacob, "the actions of our hands are in our hands."

"So?"

"So," said Jacob, "you are an adult. If you choose to do something, it's your choice, and you have no choice but to hold yourself responsible."

"Well," said the woman, less thinking about what Jacob said and more waiting for her chance to talk, "please tell me why this man I married won't love me the way I want to be loved."

"What we desperately want isn't necessarily what someone else desperately needs," said Jacob.

"What does that mean?"

"He is who he is," said Jacob. "The world is filled with men. This is the one who stepped forward, or God pushed forward, or you plucked from the crowd."

"And?"

"And," said Jacob, "he can only love you the way he can love you. But how he loves you isn't the real issue behind your heartache."

"It isn't?" asked the wife.

"The issue," said Jacob, "isn't how he loves you but how you love you."

"How I love me?"

"Yes," said Jacob. "No one can love you now the way you wanted to be loved when you were a child."

"Because?"

"Because you can't get now what you didn't get then."

"Well, would it hurt him to try?"

Jacob half laughed. "Listen, if your husband treated you now the way you wanted to be treated as a child, you would ask him, 'What are you, my father?'"

"But," said the man, "I do want to make my wife happy."

"Good," said Jacob. "But right intentions aren't always the parents of right results."

"So?"

"So, I'm sorry," said Jacob, "but it's not your work to make your wife happy. That's her work. Just like making you happy is your work."

"And that's how it works?" asked the wife.

"When it works," said Jacob, now also stamping his feet to stay warm.

"And when it doesn't?" asked the husband.

"And when it doesn't," said Jacob, "it is just work."

"What about all the lonely people?"

"Feeling alone is different from feeling lonely," said Jacob.

"I don't understand," said the wife.

"Solitude is the opposite of loneliness," said Jacob. "Solitude is the company you keep with yourself."

Together now, they asked, "And?"

"And," said Jacob, "people in love guard the solitude of the other."

"That sounds so alone," said the man.

"Not as alone as it feels if you don't like yourself," said Jacob.

"But," said the husband, "what if two lonely people meet?"

"Two lonely people," said Jacob, "don't necessarily make one happy couple."

Love is kindness regardless of the weather.

The couple continued to ignore the cold and pressed on with questions about the cold between them.

"Jacob, when we met we were so in love. What happened?"

"What grows together can also grow apart," said Jacob. "Very little begins at the beginning. Across time people can cling to what they no longer value and wind up disliking someone for the very same reason they fell in love with them."

"Do you mean hating the other person?" said the woman.

"No," said Jacob, "the opposite of love is not hate but indifference."

"But when we were young," said the man, "we promised to love each other forever."

"When you are young," said Jacob, "forever is next week."

"And what do you say?"

Jacob's own heart ached a little when he drew on his reply.

"Brief love can live long. But great love is always too short, and forgetting is never."

"So what do you suggest we do if we want to sustain this relationship?" asked the husband.

Jacob looked back at them and within himself. He spoke slowly. "Life is brief…Being kind makes us kind."

"Even when things between us grow stormy?" said the woman.

"Love," said Jacob, "is kindness regardless of the weather."

"So you're telling us that's the reason we should stay together?" asked the man.

"No," said Jacob as he turned to head home. "I'm telling you that like faith, the reason for love is not reason. When you find love, be loving."

"That's it?" asked the couple in unison.

"What else is there to say?" asked Jacob.

When you see the wind, you are watching God breathe.

Jacob sat down heavily in his reading chair and let his mind wander. The curtains, caught in the wind through the open window, lifted and fell away.

In his memory, Jacob heard his grandfather say, "When you see the wind, you are watching God breathe."

"And when the wind stops?"

"God is inhaling."

Jacob took a breath.

Then the breeze returned, and with it, his grandfather's presence.

"So many people, with so many questions, yes?"

"Yes," said Jacob.

"Remember what I told you, Grandson: 'Too many people confuse their work with their job.'"

"And we get our work until we do our work," said Jacob.

"And?"

"And our work in this life is not what we do but who we are."

"Do you understand?"

"I'm working on it," said Jacob.

"Good," said his grandfather. "And what do you tell yourself while you are working on it?"

"This is what I tell myself, Grandfather: 'You know more than you think you know, and less than you think you know. And the less you know, the more you'll learn.'"

"Getting there, getting there…" His grandfather's voice caught the wind and was inhaled into the night sky.

LITTLE MAKES US BETTER COMPANY TO OTHERS
THAN BEING GOOD COMPANY TO OURSELVES.

———

Although Jacob was not hungry, the habit of preparing an evening meal somehow kept Ruth in closer proximity. So it was understandable that as Jacob moved to the kitchen, he was startled to hear a woman's voice at his door.

"Jacob, are you home?"

He opened the door and saw a neighbor who would often offer a small wave when Jacob passed her window.

The woman's plaited hair hung over her bare shoulders.

"Hello," said Jacob, in a voice absent of any meaning.

But the woman needed no further invitation to begin. "It's just that since Ruth has passed, and you live by yourself, and I was just thinking…"

Jacob smiled guardedly.

"If you ever need anything, I'm nearby." She pointed down the road.

Jacob let the silence grow, and then said, simply, "Thank you."

"I hope I don't make you uncomfortable," said the woman.

Jacob was silent even as he paused to remind himself, *People don't do things to us; they do things for them.*

The woman could see Jacob was thinking. Hoping to draw him out, she asked, "What's on your mind?"

"Nothing," said Jacob, wrestling with his response but choosing kindness over honesty.

The woman answered with her own kindness. "Jacob, I remember you once saying what isn't said between people is also understood. And I understand."

"Thank you for being understanding," said Jacob.

"Well, I am a neighbor, and I am nearby," said the woman, now at a bit of a loss and retreating into repeating herself.

"We are all neighbors," said Jacob, "and the moments we share make us neighbors in time."

The woman nodded, half smiled, and said, "Yes, of course."

She left hastily, and Jacob went back into the house. Then he called up to Ruth as if he lived in an apartment house and heaven was simply a floor above.

"How 'bout that?"

"How 'bout it?" said Ruth.

"Do you think I was rude?"

"I think you were uncomfortable."

"I was. I am."

"Don't be."

"Don't tell me life goes on," said Jacob.

"Whether I tell you or not doesn't matter. Life goes on."

"I miss you, Ruth."

"Enjoy your life, and don't be in a rush to see me."

Jacob laughed.

"But, Jacob…"

"Yes?"

"Next time that woman knocks, tell her she should wear a shawl."

The here and now is now and here.

As Jacob had grown older, someone once asked him how he stayed current.

"What choice do I have?" answered Jacob. "In all of our lives there are currents. All of us are carried along. And along."

"That's not what I meant," said the man.

"I know," said Jacob, "but it is what we all learn."

In the current, night became day. Day became night. And time was carried downstream.

Then, one evening, after dinner, Jacob fell asleep with the book he was reading still on his lap.

Half in a dream and half-awake, he woke when he heard a rapping on one of his windows.

It was Samuel, and his nose was flattened against the glass.

Jacob laughed and opened the door.

The night was a theater of stars.

Behind Samuel were two strangers.

And while Samuel clearly had something he wanted to say, the two men had no patience for Samuel.

"Look, Jacob," said the taller of the two men, "we all agree that Ruth was the best teacher our small school ever had. And like you, we miss her greatly."

Jacob let this presumption about his loss hang insincerely in the air.

And as if the insincerity needed an echo to gain validation, the man repeated himself, this time raising his voice. "And like you, we miss Ruth greatly."

Samuel could see that Jacob was preparing to draw a curtain behind his eyes.

"Okay," said Samuel, unsure of what was beneath the surface. With love for his friend, he leavened the man's statement. "Of course no one misses Ruth like you do, we know that, but listen—"

But the shorter and stockier of strangers now pushed his way into the explanation.

"Well," said the man, hoping to set his trap. "After Ruth passed, you know we had to find another teacher, and the new teacher is young without much experience. So we thought that even after she arrives, you could come and talk with the kids at the end of the school day and answer their questions. You would also be their teacher, in the same way the children used to come and sit on the flour sacks to hear your stories at the bakery."

"Jacob," said Samuel, still the innocent, "you would be our gift to the children just like you have been a gift in all our lives."

Jacob said nothing.

Samuel took a deep breath. "So, what do you think?"

Jacob thought he could actually hear Ruth's voice urging him. "My dear, in life if you wait too long to taste your wine, you'll probably be drinking vinegar."

What Jacob said was, "I think mornings are wiser than evenings."

"He wants to think about it," said Samuel, translating Jacob to the others.

But the two schemers chose to interpret Jacob's wariness as acquiescence.

"Great," said one of the men, "so we have a deal?"

"We learn a great deal," said Jacob, looking at the two men blankly, "when we learn to deal with ourselves."

Knowing his friend, Samuel laughed.

The others didn't. The two men perhaps thought they could start a fire with wet wood if they just blew on it for long enough. "So we're good?" one said.

"Things don't have to be good for us to be great," said Jacob.

And Samuel then understood that Jacob feared something was amiss. Nothing more needed to be said.

Jacob and Samuel had been friends at every chapter in their lives. They read each other like a book. And as Samuel ushered the two men away into the night, he and Jacob turned the pages together.

> OUR DREAMS ARE POETS
> WHO WAIT UNTIL WE FALL ASLEEP
> TO FIND THEIR VOICE.

In Jacob's world, dreams were sometimes real, and reality sometimes a dream.

In this eve's dreamscape, Jacob sat quietly by a river in the timeless persona of the ferryman, watching the tide of events and taking remembered guidance from what was once whispered to him by his dreams.

> *Do not come to tell me of the long sleep ahead.*
>
> *Come instead to wake me.*
>
> *Come instead to teach me.*
>
> *Come instead so I will know*
>
> *The here and now is now and here,*
>
> *And those are blessed*
>
> *Who in your Grace*
>
> *Make rest*
>
> *From their fear.*

Jacob felt the summons of this dream in his waking life.

"Jacob."

"Yes, Ruth."

"Are you sleeping?"

"If I am, I'm dreaming of you."

"Come on, tell me, what are you thinking?"

"I'm thinking how much I wanted to thank you for all the times you waited up for me, sat up with me, and put up with me."

Jacob felt her smile's embrace.

"Jacob," asked Ruth, "tell me what you think of the community's request?"

"I trust Samuel," said Jacob.

"I hear you being guarded."

"My dear," said Jacob, "everyone draws guard duty."

"And your caution?"

"Caution's first duty," said Jacob, "is not to look out but look in. Not to guard what others will take but what we will give away."

"And...?"

"And," said Jacob, laughing, "I don't think anyone would ask me to help teach the children if they knew we were talking now."

"I'm talking; you're listening."

Jacob laughed again and felt his heart twinge. He missed his wife.

"Jacob," said Ruth, "you are the one who told me, 'If we find our fears, we have found our work, and faith is born on the other side of work.'"

"So dare to dream, but..." said Jacob.

"But plan to work," said Ruth, finishing Jacob's thought.

Jacob's eyes moistened to hear Ruth's insistence.

"And one more thing," said Ruth.

"Yes."

"Sleep in the center of the bed."

"Why?"

"Because it's time. And I like having you a little closer."

"Okay," said Jacob hesitantly.

"Are you sure?"

"No," said Jacob.

"That's okay," said Ruth.

When Jacob fell back to sleep, it was in the middle of the bed. And while he did not know for sure what he was thinking, he was not confused as to why he was smiling.

The angels looking down on Jacob were also smiling.

The angels took comfort in this man they were sent to watch over.

The updraft from this man's good work lifted them higher.

And the quiet in Jacob's home was peace.

And the moment's peace was in eternity's Grace.

And before they slipped away, the angels slipped Grace under Jacob's pillow.

Part IV

A Leap of Faith

Anyone can be right.
Wisdom is what we learn from being wrong.

―――

With beneficence propped under his pillow, Jacob woke in the company of calm and decided to take a walk by the river to think about the offer to be an adjunct teacher.

At the water's edge, Jacob watched his mind ride back and forth on the ebb and flow of yes and no.

Standing a few steps from Jacob was a boy skipping stones.

"Hey, mister," said the boy. "Did you ever do this?"

Jacob smiled as he recalled old memories.

"Were you as good as me?" asked the boy, flicking his wrist and getting a long series of skips.

"Probably not," said Jacob. "Most of my stones would sink."

"All stones sink at the end," said the boy.

"Perhaps," said Jacob, "but the smallest stone dropped in the widest sea will send radiating circles onto shores we will never know."

"Nice story, old man, but listen, here's a fact: You drop a rock, it falls."

"And here's a fact," said Jacob. "The average child will fall three hundred times before they learn to walk."

"What does that mean?"

"It means anybody standing on their own two feet has met failure before they met success."

"Get real. Failure falls flat on its face," said the boy.

"There is no ladder to success that does not have failure as a rung," said Jacob.

The boy thought on that and asked, "Mister, are you a teacher? Because the longer you talk, the more you make me feel like maybe I have a lot to learn."

"Anyone can be right," said Jacob. "Wisdom is what we learn from being wrong."

"Well, maybe," said the boy, again thinking, "but I'm sure you and I don't see the world the same way."

Jacob smiled and said, "You are wise."

"I am?" asked the boy, incredulous.

"Yes," said Jacob. "None of us see the world as it is, but as we are."

The boy looked at Jacob for a long time, then came over and stood next to him. "All right, teacher. Tell me more."

And Jacob heard Ruth say, "I told you so."

You're not young enough to know everything.

Jacob turned toward home.

And while he could feel the press of events pushing at his back for an answer, he also cautioned himself. Slowing down can sometimes be the fastest way to get somewhere. And what we don't do can sometimes be the most important thing we do.

Then, as if the universe was confirming this, Jacob heard a voice shout, "Hey, young man, slow down!"

The voice belonged to an old woman with a scarf drawn over her head. She was sitting on the front stoop of her house.

Jacob stopped and looked at her. And the woman returned the stare.

"Hey, young man," shouted the woman again, "can you hear me?"

"You had me at 'young,'" said Jacob.

"Good," said the woman, "because at my age, I don't have the time to be wrong."

"At any age," said Jacob, "it's a waste of time to spend your time needing to be right."

The woman waved him off. "Listen, kid, it takes courage to be old."

"It also takes courage to suffer happiness," said Jacob, with some of the "kid" in his voice.

Now the woman eyed him warily. "You think you know everything?"

"No," said Jacob, "I'm not young enough to know everything."

The woman thought on this and laughed.

Then she tried to stand and grudgingly accepted Jacob's offer of a hand up.

"I used to be younger," said the woman.

"Now used to be younger," said Jacob.

If we learn to laugh at ourselves, our lives will never be without amusement.

The old woman got to her feet carefully and asked, "Didn't you used to be the one they called Jacob the Baker?"

"Used to be?" asked Jacob. He ran his hands up and down his body as if checking to see he if was still alive.

"Okay," said the woman, getting the joke. "But listen to me: Every older person will at some point look at themselves and ask, 'Who's this?'"

"None of us should wait too long to ask that question," said Jacob.

"You think that's funny?" asked the woman.

"I think," said Jacob, "that if we learn to laugh at ourselves, our lives will never be without amusement."

"Okay," said the woman, "let's see if you can make me laugh."

"That depends on whether you'll be my friend," said Jacob.

"Why?"

"Because," said Jacob, "a friend is someone who will poke you with laughter when you're full of hot air."

Now the woman was laughing.

"And a real friend," said Jacob, "will tell me when I have something stuck between my teeth—like my foot."

Even as the woman now laughed, she asked, "Are you telling me to laugh more but give up on expecting more from life?"

"No," said Jacob, "but I am telling you that letting go is very different from giving up."

Luck is a strange cane.
It only serves us when we don't lean on it.

"Jacob," said the old woman, drawing closer, taking him into her confidence, "I've made a lot of mistakes."

"We've all made a lot of mistakes," said Jacob. "The challenge is to make new ones."

"And if I want to be happy?" asked the woman.

"Happy and sad are seasons," said Jacob. "Seasons change. If you doubt it, stick around."

"So?"

"So," said Jacob, "every wave that marches in, retreats."

The old woman considered this.

"The gift of living," said Jacob, "is not so much about feeling happy or sad but feeling alive in the tides that roll in and out, *and* not drowning in expectations."

"In my experience," said the woman wearily, "feelings can lead us into deep water."

"And we can drown from a life lived in the shallows," said Jacob.

"So I shouldn't worry about getting old?"

"Worry is the worst way to grow old," said Jacob.

The woman eyed him while her gears turned.

"Worry," said Jacob, "can't wait to get to sad to prove it's right."

"Come on, Jacob," said the woman, now half laughing, "you think I'm lucky to be growing old?"

"Only the lucky grow old," said Jacob.

"But," asked the woman, pointing her finger at Jacob, "can I count on being lucky?"

"My dear," said Jacob, "luck is a strange cane. It only serves us when we don't lean on it."

Memory is the secret garden.

When Jacob arrived home, he found Sophie skipping around the borders of the vegetable garden he had planted under his bedroom window.

Sophie waved at Jacob with the familiarity of a friend, welcoming him home. And Jacob waved back.

"I don't have a garden," said Sophie.

"You will."

"I will?"

"Yes. As we get older, memory is our secret garden."

"Oh," said Sophie, "I like that idea."

"Good," said Jacob. "Now that you are young, think of what you want to remember, and plant that memory in your garden for later."

"Okay, I will. Can I plant you in my garden?"

"As long as you plant me later," said Jacob, laughing heartily.

"Deal," said Sophie. "But now I want you to come with me. I want to show you something." She took Jacob's hand, tugging him to keep up with her.

"Where's your brother?" asked Jacob.

"He and the others decided I was the best for this."

"The others?" asked Jacob. But there was no reply, and the tugging continued.

"Be water," whispered Jacob's grandfather. "Sometimes to follow is to lead."

Then Sophie, as if she could read Jacob's mind, turned to him and said, "Don't you remember? It says: 'And a child shall lead them.'"

Even secret gardens need water.

It didn't take Jacob long to realize where Sophie was leading him.

He had walked this path many times with Ruth.

It was the way to the school. And at every turn in the path there were memories still tended by Jacob in his memory garden.

While uncertainty still pulled at him, Jacob reminded himself, *Sometimes we are dragged kicking and screaming to a better place.*

When they neared the school, Sophie stopped and pointed toward the front door, which was shut. "What do you see, Jacob?"

"I see a school that is empty."

"Why?"

"Because the new teacher hasn't arrived yet?"

"Nope."

"Then I don't know."

"Jacob," Sophie admonished, "I think you know that what we know can fill a book, but what we don't know can fill a library."

Jacob looked down at this little girl and marveled at her arrival in his life. Was it possible she was…?

The child stood with her small hands on her hips as if she was a teacher waiting for her student's reply.

"Okay, Sophie," said Jacob, "what do you want me to know?"

"You are here to be a source of strength to others, and the children here need you."

A moment ago Jacob was wondering if Sophie was an angel, and now he was wondering if Ruth was talking through the little girl.

"How do you know these things?" he asked her.

"I saw your heart," said Sophie.

"You saw my heart?"

"Actually I saw into your heart," said Sophie, "because your heart is open, and sort of sad."

Jacob felt his eyes moisten.

"Good," said Sophie.

"Good?" asked Jacob.

"Yes," said Sophie. "Even secret gardens need water, and tears falling on our cheeks can water our garden."

And a child shall lead them, thought Jacob.

When the student is ready, the teacher will appear— and vice versa.

———

"Come on," said Sophie again, taking Jacob's hand. "Let's just go in and look around."

Then she led Jacob to the entrance of the rustic schoolhouse.

At the front door, Jacob paused, unsure.

"This is your bakery now, Jacob the Baker," said Sophie. "This is where you are needed and where you need to be. But instead of coming early in the day to this bakery, you'll come when school is almost over, and we'll wait for you."

"Who is we?"

"All of us, all the children; it's all set."

"How do you know this?" asked Jacob.

"An angel told me," said Sophie.

"And you believe in angels?" asked Jacob.

"I believe I've met angels who don't know they're angels," said Sophie, staring intently at Jacob. "Tell me what you believe in."

Jacob was mystified. He wasn't sure just what was happening. Talking to himself as much as to Sophie, Jacob said, "My grandfather told me to believe in myself and to believe in more than myself."

"I haven't met him yet," said Sophie.

"Yet?" asked Jacob, half-stunned at how easily Sophie moved between worlds with innocence as her passport.

"Yes, yet. Will you introduce me?"

Then, without waiting for Jacob to process this answer, Sophie returned to the matter at hand. "So you'll do it?" she asked and giggled, finally sounding like a child.

Jacob heard his grandfather remind him, "Grandson, do not be confused. In this life we are a raft, not the river."

Then Ruth's insistence was also in Jacob's ear. "For heaven's sake, Jacob, just say you'll do it. Weighing something doesn't always tell us the weight of its importance."

"Yes," said Jacob, putting away the scales of decision. "I'll do it."

"Good," said Sophie, "because you're supposed to."

"Who told you that?" asked Jacob.

Sophie pointed to the heavens—stating what was for her the obvious.

Again an excited little girl burst forth from the sage-in-training, and Sophie gave a shout of glee. "Yay! Now we will all be Jacob's children."

On cue, a crowd of children, echoing Sophie's joy, scurried from behind the school, shouting and encircling Jacob.

And Jacob's heart broke tears.

And through the veil of tears, across the courtyard of time, Jacob saw his grandfather and Ruth strolling together in his memory's secret garden.

They stopped and looked at him.

"Grandson, even as you grow older, remember…"

"What grows never grows old," said Ruth.

And the two smiled at him.

And Jacob smiled back.

And together they inhaled the garden's fragrance.

THE COST FOR ANY OF US AT ANY MOMENT,
IS ALWAYS THE COST OF WHO WE ARE
AGAINST THE COST OF WHO WE MIGHT YET BE.

As Jacob moved down the path and toward his home, he found himself remembering a conversation from long ago with Jonah.

"Father, do all children feel vulnerable?"

"The sages teach us, 'All beginnings are fragile,'" said Jacob. "That is why God leans over all new life and whispers, 'Grow, grow!'"

"But as we grow and come to crossroads," asked Jonah, "what is the cost of our decisions?"

"The cost for any of us at any moment," said Jacob, "is always the cost of who we are against the cost of who we might yet be."

"But isn't how we've conducted ourselves in the past something of an addiction in all our lives?" asked Jonah.

"Yes," said Jacob, "so no matter who we are, or how old we are, we are all in recovery."

"Recovery?"

"Yes," said Jacob. "We're all recovering from who we are to become who we might be. And we should not confuse needing help with being helpless."

"And everyone who lends a hand will need a hand," chorused Jonah, fixing his gaze on Jacob.

"My son, my son," said Jacob, "thank you. Sometimes even Jacob needs Jacob."

"Yes, Father," said Jonah, already becoming a teacher to his teacher. "And even when we cannot be strong, we can still be a source of strength to others."

THE EASY PATH IS NOT ALWAYS THE EASY WAY.

———

Jacob could feel the sun on his back, and his spirit grew easy in the warmth.

Then, in counterpoint, at the curve in the road just before his home, he saw a man trapped in a dark mood.

The man grabbed for Jacob's attention. "Jacob," came the words, "I'm feeling terribly caught. I have a bad habit I need to lose."

"Old habits," said Jacob, "aren't necessarily old friends."

"So why do we keep them?"

"Because," said Jacob, "too often we prefer to live our lives doing what is negative but familiar over what is healthy but new."

"Then how do we lose these habits?"

"We can lose a habit but not the need for habits," said Jacob.

"So?"

"So the best way to change an old habit is with a new habit."

"Huh?"

"The best way to take out a thorn is with a thorn."

"You make it sound so easy."

"It's not easy," said Jacob. "But the easy path is not always the easy way."

The man sighed. "It was certainly easy to make mistakes."

"And make them a habit out of habit," said Jacob.

"Do you think I don't know this?"

"What I think," said Jacob, "is that we're all inclined to believe others don't know what we're just learning."

"And if I'm a religious person, I'm not supposed to look for the faults in others?"

"Looking for the faults in others is the wrong way to find God."

"Okay," said the man, a little confused, "but can someone like me, with faults like mine, really have any friends who can count on me changing?"

"Any of us looking for a friend without faults," said Jacob, "won't have any friends."

"So we all have faults?"

"We all have work to do."

"And where do I begin that work?"

"Look at the impossible and say, 'Why not!'"

"You think that works?" asked the man.

"If you don't confuse the impossible with the improbable," said Jacob.

"What does that mean?"

"Everything once thought impossible," said Jacob, "was also thought improbable."

"So?"

"So, the difficult must be done immediately."

"And?"

"And," said Jacob, "the impossible takes a little longer."

"How long?"

"Not how long?" said Jacob. "Just *how?*"

We are all alone.
But we are all alone together.

Jacob's single hope as he turned the last corner toward home was simply to arrive home, and still, there was someone waiting.

The man waiting for Jacob looked irritated and spoke a challenge that posed as a question.

"Jacob, I have a question for you—but please know that unlike the others who have come before you, I am not an innocent."

"We are all innocents in time," said Jacob.

"Really?"

"Yes," said Jacob. "None of us have ever arrived at any moment in our lives before that moment arrived."

"You don't believe older is wiser?"

"Sometimes."

"Sometimes?"

"If older was always wiser," said Jacob, smiling, "wisdom would be a graveyard."

"I'm not sure I agree with that."

"Good," said Jacob.

"Good?" The man was incredulous.

"Yes," said Jacob. "What many of us think of as a conflict is only something that is in conflict with what we previously thought."

"Come on, Mr. Philosopher. Give me that in a nutshell."

"Crack open any certainty," said Jacob, "and frequently you will only find a need to be certain."

"Even you do this, Jacob?"

"Like many of us," said Jacob, smiling, "I am often wrong but seldom uncertain."

Now the man was listening.

"And," said Jacob, with even more self-deprecation, "when I am wrong, I am wrong with conviction."

"So why are we so often wrong about what we think is true?"

"Because our opinions," said Jacob, "are often a self-seduction."

"What does that mean?"

"It means we welcome being seduced by what we want to believe."

The man was growing agitated. "Okay, Jacob, I'll give you a truth that's tough to swallow: Every man dies in his own arms."

"I believe you are right," said Jacob.

"Thank you," said the man.

"And you are wrong," said Jacob, holding the man's gaze.

"We are all alone," said Jacob, "but we are all alone together."

"So that means?" said the man, still uncertain.

"The alone we each know is the alone we all share," said Jacob. "The empathy for our own isolation makes us empathetic company to all others."

"And after we lose the ones we love?" asked the man.

"Tell him, Jacob," whispered Ruth.

"Those who have passed are not absent," said Jacob. "Those who have gone away are not gone. Those who pass away still pass our way. The veil between the worlds is porous."

To hear the truth,
we only have to listen for our deafness.

———

Jacob turned hesitantly at his front door when he heard footsteps.

"Please, Jacob," said an older man trying to catch his breath. "I know it is late, but I need to talk with you."

"My friend," said Jacob, looking upward. "None of us know how late it is."

The man thought on this for a moment but then rushed to his agenda. "Jacob, I need to know the best way to get someone to tell the truth."

"Give a man a mask," said Jacob, "and he'll tell you the truth."

"Did you come up with that?"

"Honestly?" asked Jacob.

The visitor laughed.

"No," said Jacob, "another man said that."

"So what do you say?"

"I say: He's right."

"Because?"

"We are often willing to trade self for company," said Jacob. "And that's always a bad trade."

"So we lie because?"

"Because we think we are getting away with something," said Jacob.

"And are we?"

"No, we are giving away something."

"What?"

"Our honesty."

"Really?"

"Honestly," said Jacob.

"Help me understand."

"What we do in the pursuit of pride will not necessarily make us proud," said Jacob. "And what we do out of fear of rejection is often only a fear of embracing our self."

"Oh," said the man, giving his mind time to sort the information.

"Any of us, at any age," said Jacob, putting his hand on the man's shoulder, "can find an excuse for what we don't want to know."

"And to hear the truth?"

"And to hear the truth," said Jacob, "we only have to listen for our deafness."

If you argue with a fool, there are two fools talking.

As the shadows lengthened, Jacob's mind returned to all the questions put before him that day.

Jacob, however, did not burden himself with being wise, but instead reminded himself: *It is only a fool who has not felt like one.*

And with this reminder, Jacob's memory traveled to yet another time when he encountered a troubled soul who began a conversation by asking for Jacob's blessing.

And to whom Jacob had replied, simply, "Peace on your roof."

"Why on my roof?"

"Because in peace," said Jacob, "there is shelter."

Still, this did not quiet the man's anxiety, and he now, more directly, prodded Jacob. "Jacob, I am often angry. Why is that?"

And Jacob answered, "When we are afraid on the inside, we're often angry on the outside."

But when the man heard this, he got angrier yet and called Jacob a fool.

On hearing this, Jacob silently turned and began to walk away.

The man grabbed Jacob and in an accusatory tone said, "Is that it? You have nothing else to say?"

"Well, my friend," said Jacob, "if you argue with a fool, there are two fools talking."

To live long, live slowly.

The season was changing, and the days were growing shorter, even as Jacob felt his days lengthening with the lines of people seeking his advice once again.

Jacob's soul counseled him to seek the company of Ruth.

So that night Jacob again followed Ruth's suggestion to sleep in the middle of the bed.

"And aren't you feeling better?" asked Ruth.

"Well," said Jacob, laughing, "at least I won't wake up on edge."

Ruth laughed.

"I miss your laugh," said Jacob.

"Do you miss my advice?" asked Ruth.

"I miss all of you," said Jacob.

"Then remember this, Jacob: To live long, live slowly. The trees that grow slowly bear the best fruit.'"

"Ahhhh," said Jacob—slowly.

"And," said Ruth, still encouraging Jacob to be Jacob, "to get the fruit in life, you sometimes have to go out on a limb."

And in the middle of the bed, in the middle of the night, Jacob counted his blessings. On his roof.

Part V

Hope Is Its Own Reality

Not everyone who is crying is crying out loud.

By now, many in the community had heard about the new teacher and Jacob's invitation to teach the children after school. And with this news came attendant questions.

"We all have expectations about the new teacher," said a woman. "Don't you, Jacob?"

"We want to be cautious," said Jacob, "of making our expectations someone else's burden."

"Well," said the woman, "I'm sure you agree that God never gives us more than we can bear."

"Many of our burdens," said Jacob, "are not God given."

"What does that mean?"

"Very often," said Jacob, "little weighs heavier on us than who we are."

"Yes, but…" said the woman.

"Yes, but," said Jacob, "and sometimes, life does give us more than we can bear."

Those crowding Jacob were listening closely now.

"Any of us," said Jacob, "can fall under the burdens that fall on us or we bring to bear in our lives. And no one needs to have our expectations of what they can bear as an additional burden."

"But," asked the woman, "won't people tell us if they are under too great a load?"

"Sadly," said Jacob, "not everyone who is crying is crying out loud."
"Oh, Jacob," said the woman, "just to hear that makes me cry."
"Sometimes," said Jacob, "the best of us are washed in tears."

Parents have as much
responsibility to be students
as they do teachers.

―

Many years before, when Jacob was a boy and expressed uncertainty to his grandfather, he remembered his grandfather saying, "No one has ever arrived at certitude who hasn't traveled through doubt. But be cautious of being self-wounding; doubt is the pain before the wound."

Jacob now witnessed the truth in this advice. And how broad and deep the community of doubt was in every community.

Many in Jacob's community, seeing that even after his loss of Ruth, he was still Jacob and realized how much they valued him, and drew their circle of doubts and questions even more tightly around him.

"We heard there is a new teacher in the community," said a woman, "but don't you know more than the new teacher?"

"I don't want to jeopardize what I will learn," said Jacob, "with what I think I already know."

"And parents? Shouldn't parents have a major influence on their children?"

"It is important that we allow our children the time to learn who they are," said Jacob, "before we insist they become who we are."

"Still," asked someone else, "isn't it the right of parents to teach their children?"

"Of course," said Jacob. "Rights, however, are born with responsibilities. And parents have as much responsibility to be students as they do teachers."

"Students of our children?"

"What we learn," said Jacob, "is more important than where we learn it."

"But from children?"

"We are all God's children," said Jacob.

"These are children—not angels."

And Jacob answered, "All God's children have wings."

Fear is where courage is born.

Now, a man, speaking almost in a whisper, asked, "Jacob, why does the anguish experienced by children so often pass from generation to generation?"

"Sadly," said Jacob, "children raised without self-worth cannot value themselves, and people who cannot value themselves cannot value others."

"And that's how it goes?"

"That's how it goes wrong," said Jacob.

"Help me understand."

"Just as a woman one day puts her arm in a sweater and out comes her mother's hand, the going-away gifts we give our children—of hurt or health—they will give to their children, and their children's children."

"So what do we tell children who have been wronged?"

Jacob paused on this question, then speaking slowly, said, "Just because you were wronged, that doesn't make *you* wrong. Don't confuse what happened to you with who you are."

"That's hard to do," said the man, half confessing his own anguish.

"You are right," said Jacob, "but while victims can't heal the past, they don't have to live there."

"Where, then, do we tell this child to live emotionally?"

Seeing a child's pain in the adult's eyes, Jacob said, "Moving on is the only direction life moves. Look to the future because that's where you will live."

"But what if I'm afraid to begin that journey?"

"To win we must begin. Fear is where courage is born," said Jacob.

"And what if I'm afraid that my fears are too powerful?"

"Our fears," said Jacob, "only have the power we give them."

Even a broken clock is right twice a day.

Two men who were at odds about something sought Jacob's attention.

"Jacob," said the first man, "I say that even a sage who speaks long enough is going to say something foolish."

"And I say," said the second man, "even a fool who speaks long enough will say something wise."

Jacob simply nodded, and then replied, "You are both right."

A woman who strained to overhear the conversation asked, "How can he be right and he be right?"

And Jacob answered, "Okay, you're right too."

IN EACH OF US THERE IS A BETTER PERSON
WE TOO OFTEN CONFUSE WITH SOMEONE ELSE.

———

A woman standing apart from the crowd pressed in and said, "Jacob, I know you are wise, but where will I find wisdom?"

Jacob laughed. "For any of us to find wisdom, we only have to go in search of our ignorance."

"Even you, Jacob?"

"In each of us there is a better person we too often confuse with someone else."

"Why don't we meet our better person?"

"We're waiting to be introduced."

"Why the delay?"

"Too often," said Jacob, "we prefer to be someone who is less than our best but familiar to us rather than someone who is better but new to us."

"Is that a fault?"

"Perhaps not," said Jacob, "but it is certainly an opportunity."

"And if I don't take that opportunity?"

"Time is indifferent," said Jacob. "It will take you just the way you are."

"And my life will be over?"

"Over and over again," said Jacob.

"That's sad," said the woman.

"What's sad," said Jacob, "is when we forget that being sad or happy is more often a choice than an obligation."

"Do we really have a choice?"

"How you answer that question," said Jacob, "is your choice."

It's not what you're thinking, but how you're thinking it.

———

A man, looking both agitated and confused, rushed up to Jacob. "I'm upset with myself because I get angry too often."

"Anger is a distraction," said Jacob.

"From what?"

"From what made you angry."

"Are you telling me there's something I'm not dealing with?"

"What I'm telling you," said Jacob, "is that to find the real gold in life you have to mine yourself."

"But sometimes I get angry just like I get hungry."

"And many times," said Jacob, "our hunger has nothing to do with being hungry. Many of us who feel we are starving are starving for self-affection or self-respect."

"But what about when things don't go the way I want?"

"Adversity," said Jacob, "sharpens the knife."

"And what if adversity makes me feel like I'm a nobody?"

"We're all nobodies," said Jacob. "And every nobody is somebody special."

"That's not what I think," said the man.

"Unfortunately," said Jacob, "many of us know what we're thinking but not how we're thinking it."

"But how does *how* I'm thinking have to do with *what* I'm thinking?"

Jacob smiled. "What does the size of your foot have to do with the size of your shoe?"

Killing time is the worst form of littering.

While many who waited to see Jacob or stopped him in the street came burdened with the large issues in life, Jacob was fond of reminding himself: *The small problems we avoid are often the next crisis we invent.*

He was considering this when a man who was lingering nearby said, "Just so you know, I don't have a question for you. I'm just killing a little time."

"Don't litter," said Jacob, quite seriously.

"I'm not littering," said the man.

"Oh, but you are," said Jacob.

The man chuckled. "I told you, I'm just waiting here, killing a little time."

"Killing time is throwing away moments," said Jacob, "and that is the worst form of littering."

"Why do you say that?"

"In the moment before someone you love passes away, or in the moment before you pass away," said Jacob, "ask me that question again."

Change is the way the river runs.
Progress is when we change the way we run.

———

A woman whose features were as sharp edged as her manner elbowed someone aside and grabbed Jacob's arm.

"Jacob," said the woman, "people tell me I am too judgmental. But can you tell me what's wrong about judging others?"

"Being too judgmental can make us a thief," said Jacob.

"Stealing from who?"

"From ourselves!"

"How?"

"When we spend a great deal of time judging others," said Jacob, "it robs us of the brief time we're allotted to be accepting of others."

"And you think knowing this will make my life more?"

"Not knowing this," said Jacob, "will make your life less."

"But accepting can be difficult."

"Of course accepting can be difficult, because our ability to be accepting of others requires us to be self-accepting—just as our ability to love others requires us to be self-loving."

"Come on, Jacob," said the woman, "that's just common sense."

"Common sense is not that common," said Jacob.

The woman thought on that for a moment and then asked, "Okay then, what does uncommon sense say is the difference between change and progress?"

"Change is the way the river runs," said Jacob. "Progress is when we change the way we run."

Be self-accountable, not self-abusive.

A friend of the woman in conversation with Jacob now grabbed her chance and asked, "Okay, so here's my question, Jacob. And I just want a simple answer because this is a question a lot of us ask ourselves. How can we make the changes we want in who we are?"

"All the major portals we travel through in life—love, parenting, age, illness, fame, failure—less transform us than reveal us," said Jacob. "So, all personal transformation requires self-witnessing."

"You make it sound like I should put myself on trial."

"You are not on trial, but life can be a trial, and we all need to tell ourselves the truth, the whole truth, and nothing but the truth."

"And if I judge myself to be doing something wrong, I should do what?"

"Be self-accountable," said Jacob.

"You mean beat myself up?" asked the woman.

"No," said Jacob. "Do not confuse being self-abusive with being self-accountable."

"Wait a minute!" pressed the woman. "When I get angry with myself because of something I've done, why shouldn't I punish myself?"

When Jacob answered, his voice was as patient as it was insistent.

"Sadly," said Jacob, "too many of us were raised to think that beating ourselves up is an act of character."

"It's not?"

"No," said Jacob. "Character is more than the triumph of self-defeat. And beating yourself up is catharsis without progress."

"Is that true for any of us at any age?"

"Tell a child they are a fool for long enough," said Jacob, "and you will be a prophet."

Over every finish line in life are the words, "Begin here!"

Sighing heavily as he spoke, a man measuring his words said, "You know, Jacob, sometimes you are a little confusing."

"The wise," said Jacob, "tell us that if we're not confused, we're not thinking clearly."

"Are you saying there are no answers, Jacob?"

"Oh, there are answers…but there are no final answers."

"Are you sure?"

"What I'm sure of is that every sunset is a sunrise somewhere."

"That sounds trite."

"Sometimes," said Jacob, "the truth is trite."

"I'm sorry, but things aren't that simple."

"The complicated is a simplicity we have not yet solved," replied Jacob. "No one can tell the time by looking inside a clock."

"But," said the man, wanting to make his point, "surely there are finish lines in life."

"Yes," said Jacob. "And over every finish line in life, are the words, 'Begin here!'"

In each of us there is a place where we are better than our fears.

"Jacob," said a new voice with insistence, "sometimes when you talk, I think you are in a dialogue with yourself."

"What any of us say to others," said Jacob, "is something we need to hear—a line we toss to ourselves when we're in water over our heads."

"Are you sure?"

"What I'm sure of," said Jacob, "is that every line extended far enough into the heavens turns back on itself."

"You think so?"

Jacob laughed. "Science thinks so."

"Does that mean that the fears we don't want to face will turn to face us?"

"All fears return to roost from where they flew," said Jacob.

"So?"

"So, fears follow doubt," said Jacob, "and faith follows hope."

"And your suggestion?" asked the voice.

"Doubt your fears; have faith in hope," said Jacob.

"Because?"

"Because," said Jacob, "in each of us is a place where we are better than our fears."

No one can take your good deeds, and no one tries to steal your troubles.

Unsure why, one morning Jacob remembered a joke that Ruth liked to tell about a man who stayed up all night to see if he snored.

And while Jacob laughed, he thought the same was true: If you watched the dawn, the darkness without end departed without announcing its leaving.

And time was passing, and by now, it was clear to all that one no longer had to go to the bakery if one wanted to speak with Jacob the Baker. And so the questions found him and surrounded him.

"Tell me, Jacob," asked a man who had come a great distance. "What do you think it means to be inspired?"

"The word 'inspired,'" said Jacob, "means to be filled with breath. And since it is written that the first human being was born from the breath of God...and since no living soul can take a breath without releasing their breath...then all breath, every breath ever breathed, is still shared by all."

"So?"

"So," said Jacob, "since every breath we take is in some way the borrowed first breath from God, we are all divinely inspired."

"Whew," said the man, exhaling as he thought about this.

"Of course," said Jacob, "this also means that when we inhale and exhale, we are in God's company. So everyone is inspired by *and* conspiring with God."

"I don't understand."

"To be a conspirator," said Jacob, "means to breathe together, and everyone who is breathing is together breathing God's first breath. Which also means that with every inhalation, we are in a state of spiritual resuscitation."

The man just stood there looking at Jacob for a moment and then said, "Jacob, do you ever think you're an angel, and no one can see your wings?"

Jacob shied from the question but replied, "My friend, I have learned that life's journey is about the heroic dignity of those who carry on in life without wings."

"Carry on in what way?"

"Often in life," said Jacob, "we can feel profoundly blessed and profoundly sad, simultaneously. And the challenge, at any point in our life, is to be fully alive in both of these moments at the same moment."

The man fell silent, and then asked, "Jacob, what else have you learned that I will be more at peace for knowing?"

"No one can take your good deeds, and no one tries to steal your troubles."

"Did an angel tell you that?"

"Yes," said Jacob, "a very real angel: my wife."

Part VI

Finding the Door

Prayer is a path where there is none.

———

An old man had once asked Jacob, "Can you tell me the difference between a house and a coffin?"

And Jacob answered, "The difference between a house and coffin is a door."

"I don't understand," said the man.

"A door," said Jacob, "is a hole we cut in our walls."

"And the door between this world and the next," asked the man, "is it a push or pull?"

"The door is indifferent," said Jacob. "Find the door."

"And if I can't find the door?" asked the man.

"Be the door," said Jacob.

"How is that possible?"

"We are led in one door and led out another," said Jacob. "To be lost is impossible."

Now, on the day he was to meet the new teacher, as Jacob opened his door, he stopped and turned back inside. Then he reminded himself that to see the truth, a man only had to go in search of his blindness.

Jacob placed his right foot on the doorstep, so he got off on the right foot, touched the doorframe with two fingers, and found prayer.

Here was his ritual on arriving and leaving his home, and his reminder that God lived in this house.

The habit of this act was not lost in its habit.

"Prayer is a path where there is none," said Jacob to himself, "and ritual is prayer's chariot."

It is a wonder to grow old
if we grant our wonder
the right to be born again.

———

When Jacob pulled the door open, the door in the moment opened.

Then his grandfather's spirit pushed in from the other side, gained entrance, and offered this counsel:

"Grandson, every journey has its own journey; intention is rarely destination.

"Remember to be cautious of those who confuse the power of love with a love of power.

"Remember that getting older doesn't make you wise any more than getting sick makes you a saint.

"And remember that the true measure of a community is how people with power treat people without power."

Jacob listened, touched his heart, and giving wings to respect, looked up.

"Now hurry up," said his grandfather. "Remember, only God owns; the rest of us rent."

"I promise not to forget," said Jacob.

"Good," said his grandfather proudly, "because you have promise."

At this, Jacob laughed out loud.

Then he looked into the bright blue of the day, bowed his head, and wrapped himself in the moment's prayer shawl of peace.

It is a wonder to grow old, thought Jacob, *if we grant our wonder the right to be born again.*

Our grasp is only exceeded by what can slip between our fingers.

As Jacob approached the school, he was sure he could feel Ruth's hand pushing him on.

At one point he was so convinced of this, he stopped, looked up, and asked, "Are you worried I will be late to school?"

And Ruth answered, "If you are late, I'm not writing you a note."

Jacob arrived at the school before the children. The new teacher sat at her desk preparing her lesson. She did not hear him enter. When she looked up, she seemed a little startled.

"Excuse me," said the young woman, as she tried to get her bearings, "school hasn't started yet."

"Really?" asked Jacob. "I was of a mind that school was always in session, but students were not always present."

"Okay, okay," she said, putting down her pencil. She quickly calmed herself and spoke in a manner older than her years. "I know who you are."

"Well," said Jacob, "I would appreciate the introduction." He smiled and extended his hand. "My name is Jacob."

She laughed and accepted his hand. Then she pointed to the door. "The children won't be here for a while."

"Tomorrow, I will meet the children. Today, I came to meet you."

"That wasn't necessary. The community made it clear to me that you would be the children's teacher at the close of the day. And I have no problem with that."

"I came to meet you," said Jacob, "because I was hoping that you would also be my teacher."

She blushed. "I hardly think it's possible for me to teach someone like you."

"Really?" said Jacob. "As a teacher, don't you think every student has promise?"

She laughed again and said, "Even I have grasped that everyone knows of your wisdom."

Jacob let the praise slide off him before he replied.

"What any of us can grasp," said Jacob, "is only exceeded by what can slip between our fingers."

Hope is a friend we can all turn to.

———

The teacher was concerned that she had not really introduced herself to Jacob.

"My name is Elizabeth."

"A beautiful name," said Jacob.

"It means 'God's promise.'"

"And I promise to be respectful in your house."

Jacob looked around the one-room schoolhouse, half imagining he could still see Ruth behind the desk.

"I'm hoping we'll be friends," said Elizabeth.

"Hope is a friend we can all turn to," said Jacob.

"I'm learning that," said Elizabeth, smoothing her dress and knowing she was giving away a little of herself even as she said it.

"We're all learning that," said Jacob.

"So you don't think I'm not old enough to be a teacher?"

"My thoughts are just the opposite," said Jacob.

"The opposite?"

"Yes," said Jacob. "I'm concerned for those who confuse getting older with being old."

"Jacob, I hope you don't mind me saying this, but people think you're great."

"Great men, great flaws," said Jacob.

Elizabeth smiled.

"However," said Jacob, smiling back, "great flaws are not necessarily a sign of great men."

Those who live on the edge, grow wings.

———

Having met the new teacher, and not wanting to interrupt her preparations, Jacob prepared to leave.

Elizabeth, however, felt a confession was necessary. "Jacob, please forgive me for appearing so startled by your presence. It's just that I am new to teaching and feel like I'm standing on the edge of a cliff."

Jacob's reassured her: "Those who live on the edge, grow wings."

"Then I'll be okay?"

"You will soar."

"And if I'm a little scared?"

"We're all a little scared," said Jacob. "Fears grow in every garden. Water your faith."

"This is all so new for me," said Elizabeth. "I only recently moved here, was suddenly offered this job, and wonder what I've left behind."

"Every great adventure," said Jacob, "begins with a farewell."

"Perhaps, but this is a new world for me."

"You will be fine," said Jacob. "A leap of faith is every pilgrim's first step."

"Thank you for caring," said Elizabeth.

"Caring heals the healer," said Jacob.

"How is that possible?" asked Elizabeth.

"Caring is prayer," said Jacob.

"Amen," said Elizabeth, surprising even herself at how quickly that came out.

Jacob walked to the door but paused as he remembered something.

He returned to the teacher's desk, stood next to her, and handed her a slip of paper.

She opened her hand to receive it.

He folded her hands over the note and walked away.

Elizabeth just stood there, not sure what to make of this and not wanting to open her hand.

Confused, she looked toward Jacob, and asked, "Why?"

"Because," said Jacob, turning at the door, "when we open our hearts to others, we offer blessings a place to land in our life."

Don't let the past kidnap your future.

Elizabeth ate her evening meal slowly and set down her fork.

She needed to think.

She found her mind still turning over the things Jacob had said.

The note he left her was now resting on the table next to her. She wanted it close.

She so wished she could talk with her father, she imagined herself into a conversation with him.

And yet, when her father said, "Hello, my dear," Elizabeth was stunned.

"I can't believe you're here."

"Believe it," he said. "You look like you're doing a lot of thinking."

She smiled and said, "I am…I miss you, Dad."

"I got the message. Talk to me."

"The man everyone calls Jacob the Baker came by before school to say hello."

"Tell me more," said her father.

"Well, ever since I've arrived, I've heard people talking about Jacob the Baker. Their voices even change when they mention his name. He's like a sage or scholar but a very simple man, and compassionate. I actually think his compassion *is* his real wisdom."

"That's a lot for a man to be," said her father.

"You ought to know," said Elizabeth. She looked through the veil of time and into her father's eyes.

"What did this Jacob say to you?"

"He said he hoped I would be his teacher."

"The sage asked you to be his teacher?"

"Yes."

"I already like this guy."

"Really?"

"Absolutely. If he's wise enough to want you for a teacher, I want to meet him."

"You can. I mean you could if you were here."

"But I am here, with you. You know that."

"I know."

"And?" asked her father.

"And some in the town have asked him to be a teacher to the children who want to stay after school and learn from him."

"And the children go along with this?"

"The children are among the most encouraging."

"Let me get this straight. The children are going to stay after school to sit and learn from Jacob?"

"Yes," said Elizabeth, nodding slowly.

"You think he's that special?"

"I do, but he doesn't."

"Is he old?"

She thought on that for a moment. "Not old. More timeless."

"Come on."

"When the town council asked me to be the teacher and told me about Jacob, I asked the same question."

"And what did they say?"

"They told me Jacob's wife described him as a two-thousand-year-old teacher temporarily inhabiting the body of a younger man."

"Did she pass recently?"

"Not that long ago."

"How is he dealing with that?"

"I think he still draws water from a well of sadness."

"Sometimes we all drink at that well."

"I know," said Elizabeth, "but…"

"But what?"

"Well, when I was interviewing for the job, one of the men on the council said that Jacob told him, 'Telling people why they shouldn't be sad doesn't necessarily make them happy.'"

"He's right."

"And one of the children in my class said Jacob told her mother, 'Sadness is a season and seasons change.'"

"Right as rain."

And Elizabeth opened her hand as if anticipating the first drops.

The moment paused and passed, and then…

"So?" asked her father, urging his daughter along.

"So," said Elizabeth, "I thought Jacob would understand some of my fears about this new job. And I was going to ask him how I could calm my fears, but…"

"But what?"

"It was like he knew my question without me asking it. And when he was leaving, Jacob handed me a slip of paper with a note written on it. Then he closed my hand around it and walked away."

"And what did the note say?"

"It said: 'Don't let the past kidnap your future.'"

Silence.

"What do you make of that, Dad?"

"I think it is a complicated world down there, and you've made a wise and gentle friend."

"I think so too, but something in me worries a little for him."

"I understand," said her father, "but I don't think you have to worry. I just heard there are angels watching over him."

Now Elizabeth was fully stunned. "How do you know that?"

"I told you. Word gets around up here."

"Come on, Dad!"

"Elizabeth, there are fewer secrets in life than you might think. The secret is to listen to them."

Sadness and joy can fly—away.

The two beds sat in whispering distance.

Sophie was already in bed when her brother slid into the matching bed next to hers.

"Jacob is going to be at school tomorrow," whispered Sophie.

"How do you know?" asked Caleb.

"The teacher told me. She said he came by to meet her."

"Do you have a question you want to ask Jacob?"

"I have lots of questions," said Sophie.

"You usually have a lot of answers," said Caleb, poking his sister a little.

"You're right," said Sophie, "but we're talking about Jacob."

"I've got a question," said her brother.

"Tell me."

"I want to ask him what you do when your dreams don't come true."

"Are you sad, Caleb?"

"A little."

"Sometimes I'm sad," said Sophie, and the confession seemed to draw their beds even closer.

"Why don't you ask Jacob what he does when he's sad?"

The children's mother opened the door slightly. "It's bedtime. What are you two talking about?"

The children didn't answer.

"Tell me," said their mother.

"Jacob," said Sophie.

"And what we want to ask him tomorrow," said Caleb.

"I don't want to hear any more about Jacob tonight," said their mother.

The children's father stood behind his wife and pushed the door open a little wider. "And I don't want to hear any more about Jacob any night. Just say good night!"

The children exchanged looks and then quietly said, "Good night."

In the dark, Sophie reached out. "Caleb, will you please hold my hand for a few minutes?"

Caleb extended his hand, found his sister's hand, grasped it gently, and said, "Sometimes I'm more than a little sad."

They could hear their parents arguing about Jacob, and "What do you think he's going to be teaching these kids?"

Sophie and Caleb fell asleep to the sound of the argument outside their room. And their spirits fell with them.

And they were alone together.

Part VII

We Are All Jacob's Children

Wisdom is where we are wise enough to find it.

It was Jacob's first day as a teacher.

Thinking on this brought him back to his own first day at school and going there with his grandfather.

Even now, Jacob could still remember the soft, leathery feel of the old man's hand and could still hear the conversation across time.

"Jacob, honesty is the door to all wisdom, but humility is the door to all honesty."

"And, Grandfather," said Jacob, "don't the sages teach us we're not expected to finish our work, but neither are we excused from it?"

The old man smiled. "Yes, and working on who we are is life's labor, so make it a labor of love."

"So to find our way," said Jacob, "we are wiser to follow the path with a heart."

"And when you pray…?"

"Pray less *please* and more *thank you*," said Jacob, "because gratitude is the portal to prayer."

Then Jacob's grandfather looked down at Jacob with the pale-blue eyes Jacob knew as his own.

"My grandson, before I leave you at the school's door, remind me—where do we find wisdom?"

And Jacob answered, "Wisdom is where we are wise enough to find it."

The old man ran his hand through the boy's hair and said nothing more.

And the nothing more was all that needed to be said.

Tears falling on our cheeks can cause us to bloom.

―――

When he arrived at the school, Jacob felt that for the first time in a long time he was sailing not into the wind but with the wind.

Elizabeth was waiting at the door. "The children are expecting you."

"Thank you," said Jacob. "I won't keep them late."

"I think the problem will be getting them to leave."

Caleb and Sophie suddenly appeared on both sides of Elizabeth.

Neither Jacob nor Elizabeth said anything for a moment. Then Elizabeth put a key in Jacob's hand.

"It's the key to the school. I thought you should have one."

"You are the key to the school," said Jacob.

Elizabeth was touched—and then immediately self-conscious.

"Will you stay?" asked Jacob.

"I will, but I'll sit in the back of room. After all, we are all Jacob's children."

"You see," said Sophie, "we told her, and she remembered."

Then Elizabeth leaned forward and touched Jacob's face. The kindness of the gesture caught Jacob completely by surprise.

"Thank you for the note you left me."

Now it was Jacob's turn to feel self-conscious.

The children were giggling and began calling to Jacob, trying to draw his attention.

Well, Ruth, asked Jacob inwardly, *any thoughts?*

Ruth said, "I think Jacob's children are waiting for him."

I think I've been waiting for them, thought Jacob.

"Time can heal what is broken," said Ruth.

"And break what is left waiting," said Jacob to himself, with a penetrating sadness still calling on him.

"Yes, my dear Jacob," whispered Ruth, "but the man I still love once told me that 'tears falling on our cheeks can also cause us to bloom.'"

Of all the things you can make in life, why not make a difference?

Jacob entered the classroom and sat down, slowly, almost comically, in one of the small chairs next to the children.

The children laughed as he squeezed into the seat.

And without any further invitation, the questions began.

"Didn't you used to be a baker?"

"Yes," said Jacob, "but we only have two arms. If we're busy hugging the past, we can't embrace the future."

Then a boy, almost smirking, asked, "Jacob, were you sad when you did something you knew wasn't very nice?"

"Sure," said Jacob, "but then I told myself God wasn't done with me yet."

"I don't like my new little sister," said a girl, sticking her tongue out.

"Well, one day she won't be your new little sister," said Jacob. "One day, when you're much older, she will be the sister who sits down slowly—probably very slowly—next to you on a bench in the park, and you will laugh together about how you used to stick out your tongue at her."

"Will she remember that?"

"Let me see your tongue," said Jacob.

The girl stuck out her tongue and laughed.

Jacob peered at her as if inspecting the girl's tongue, and said, "Oh, your sister will remember."

Everyone in the class laughed.

"How 'bout me?" asked another child. "Will I make a lot of money?"

"Maybe," said Jacob. "But of all the things you can make in life, why not make a difference?"

"But there's nothing wrong with making money?" asked a boy.

"Nothing's wrong with making money," said Jacob. "But you only have one life to spend. So be careful what you spend it on."

"Still," said the boy, "what about people who say if you give money to poor people you will be poor?"

Jacob answered slowly and quietly. "No one ever became poor by giving."

"Who said that?" asked the boy.

"A little girl," said Jacob, "in her diary."

"When?"

"When she didn't think anyone would read it."

For the first time since Jacob's arrival, there was a silence in the room.

"Jacob," asked Sophie, who had been waiting for a pause, "have you ever had a dream that didn't come true?"

"Yes," said Jacob, and the abruptness of his answer caught her off guard.

"Did you cry?"

"Yes."

"Because your dream didn't come true?"

"Sometimes we cry," said Jacob, "because our dreams don't come true. And sometimes we cry because our dreams do come true."

"So what should we do?"

"The greatest challenge in life," said Jacob, his eyes moving from one child to the other, "is daring to be who you are."

"And what should we do when we grow up?" asked Sophie.

"The greatest opportunity in life," said Jacob, "is daring to be the person you might yet become."

You are the paint, the painter, and the painting.

———

As the children invited Jacob into their questions, he drew them out.

"Jacob," said a girl sitting just to the side of the others, "I want to be an artist."

"Great," said Jacob. "Make your life a work of art."

"I mean I want to be a painter."

"Great," said Jacob. "Make your life a work of art, and know you are the paint, the painter, and the painting."

"Jacob," said the little girl, "I mean I really want to create things."

"Will you sign what you create?" asked Jacob.

"Of course," said the child proudly.

"Good," said Jacob, "but understand that the only label we all wear says, 'Handmade by God.'"

This had the children thinking. And the questions continued.

"I heard that artists need a good imagination," said a girl in the back of the room. "Is it hard to have imagination?"

"For many people," said Jacob, "the hardest part of imagining is giving yourself permission to imagine."

The children's eyes darted around at this idea. And as the words now spilled from Jacob, the children's eyes got bigger and bigger.

"Imagine," said Jacob, "that to imagine was not a to-do list but a to-be list.

"Imagine that to imagine made you more than a poet—it made you poetry.

"Imagine that to imagine allows you to dream: *yes, you can*; *yes, you will.*"

"Jacob," said a boy in the front row, "you make imagination sound like a dream machine."

"Imagine that," said Jacob.

In "Once upon a time," God is time.

The children were still; their imaginations were not.

One of the younger girls came forth tentatively, tapped Jacob's knee, and said, "Jacob, I like that you don't speak down to us just because we are little."

"I think you make us taller," added another girl, "because you make us stand on our toes to reach your ideas."

And Jacob said, "No matter what you are reaching for in life, reaching out to others is a great way to stretch."

"Jacob," said a boy in the back row, "do you think kids need to hear fairy tales?"

"I think we all need to hear fairy tales," said Jacob.

"Why?"

"So we can understand what we need to know about things we are afraid to know," said Jacob.

"Why?"

"Because," said Jacob, "life is not a fairy tale."

Elizabeth, who was clearly caught up in the back-and-forth, suddenly heard herself ask a question. "Jacob, every fairy tale begins the same way, but where is God in 'Once upon a time'?"

"Ah," said Jacob, turning toward her with a smile. "In 'Once upon a time,' God is time."

"Some people say God is a fairy tale," said a young boy who had inched closer.

"And for some people," said Jacob, "a fairy tale is what they call something so they can give themselves permission not to believe it."

Then Jacob touched his heart and extended his hand toward all the children. "And I believe I will see you tomorrow."

"But what is our homework tonight?" asked one of the girls.

"Tonight, dear child," said Jacob, "your homework is to climb aboard your imagination, and set sail on 'Once upon a time…'"

"And then what?" asked several of the children.

"And then…" Jacob's voice lilted into a lullaby…

"Row, row, row your boat,
Gently down the stream,
Merrily, merrily, merrily, merrily,
Life is but a dream."

And the small school and all Jacob's children sailed on.

Honesty is the door to all wisdom; humility is the door to all honesty.

That evening, when Jacob lay the day down to sleep, he remembered once waking and finding a note next to his bed that he had no memory of writing.

The note read, "I write things wiser than I am."

If someone had asked Jacob if the pursuit of wisdom required humility, he would have said yes.

If they asked him how long that journey was, he would have said, "I don't know."

Jacob folded humility into his pillow, leaned into the crease, turned, and went to sleep.

All private deceit eventually becomes public deceit.

———

The next afternoon, when Jacob left to be with the children, a man was waiting with his questions but had to run after Jacob to stay close.

"Jacob," the man half shouted, "I have to ask you something."

"I need to be at the school," said Jacob.

"I'll write you a note."

Jacob liked that and stopped. He thought he could see Ruth smiling.

"Listen, Jacob," said the man, "I did something recently that makes me feel embarrassed."

"Embarrassment," said Jacob, "is the distance between who we want to think we are and who we learn we are."

"But…" said the man, trying to see where this was going.

"But," said Jacob, "others can't find out anything about us that we don't already know."

"So what should I do?"

"You need a second opinion."

"From who?"

"From you."

"Because I lied to others?"

"Because you lied to yourself."

"So?"

"So," said Jacob, "you need to give yourself an opinion on who you are that isn't based on the fear or expectation of what others will think."

"Help me understand."

"When we hide something from ourselves," said Jacob, "this is a private deceit. But there is no private deceit."

"Why?"

"Because," said Jacob, "who we are in the dark is who we will eventually be in the light."

"So?"

"So," said Jacob, "all private deceit eventually becomes public deceit."

"Really?"

"Trust me. What we hide from, we will also hide from others. And we all trespass on ourselves before we are caught by others. So when we cheat on others, we cheat ourselves of the best in us."

The man just stood there with his head nodding. And then he asked, "Hey, Jacob, just one more thing."

"Yes," said Jacob, already turning to head toward the school.

"Can you find me a seat in that classroom?"

Honest confusion can be honest prayer.

The man who hoped for a place in Jacob's classroom was not alone.

As the school now became Jacob's regular destination, people in the community, and those who traveled far to seek out Jacob's guidance, knew exactly where to find him.

And while Jacob knew the children were waiting, and did not want to be delayed, when he saw an old woman standing by the side of the road near the school, he stopped. He could read the trouble in her soul and the need to connect.

The woman waved Jacob over. "I've been planning how to catch up with you," she said.

And Jacob answered, "My mother used to say, 'If you want to give God a good laugh, tell Her your plans.'"

The woman almost laughed, but then quickly returned to her purpose. "Jacob, I really need to talk with you."

Diminishing his own importance, Jacob said, "Too many of us confuse what we don't need with something we must have."

Now the woman did laugh, but only for a moment. "I have a problem," she said, "that you may understand."

"None of us can be certain we know the weight of what is weighing on others," said Jacob, motioning that the woman should continue.

"Jacob," said the woman, with a painful slowness, "I want to ask you a question about losing someone you love."

Jacob was silent.

The woman took the silence as further invitation.

"My husband is in pain and dying. And I am very confused. I don't know whether to ask God to take the man I love or to extend his life."

"Honest confusion can be honest prayer," said Jacob.

The woman's eyes now moved between pain and uncertainty.

"This is not a decision between you and God," said Jacob, "but between your husband and God."

"And I can't say anything?"

"Of course you can. You can tell God how good a man your husband is and how much you love him."

"And?"

"And you can ask heaven to show compassion."

"And have faith?" asked the woman.

"Don't have faith; be of faith," said Jacob. "Prayer knocks on God's door. Faith moves in."

"That's a big step for someone who feels so helpless."

"In life we too often confuse what we can do to help with what we can do to be in control."

"So I'm helpless?"

"You are not helpless," said Jacob, "but neither are you in charge."

"Still, I feel I should do something more."

"Do your best; make peace with the rest."

"How can I make peace with the rest?"

"Wage peace."

"How can I do that?"

"As with faith, the only way to wage peace is to be peace," said Jacob.

"And if I wonder where God is?"

"God," said Jacob, "is in the wonder."

OUR SOUL DOES NOT BEAR THE BURDEN OF OUR BODY.

"Jacob," said the woman, struggling to deal with the prospect of her husband's passing, "do you really think that hope can influence events?"

"I think prayer is hope with wings," said Jacob.

"Meaning?" asked the woman.

"Prayer is the shortest distance between hope and faith."

"I don't know if I can get there from here."

"In a state of faith here is there!" said Jacob.

"Even now?"

"The here and now is now and here," said Jacob, remembering his own poet's dream.

"If you are telling me that to get to faith takes faith, you are not being reasonable," said the woman.

"Faith is not a journey that reason can make or wants to take," said Jacob.

"Why?"

"Because," said Jacob, "reason requires our mind to take one step at a time, but the first step to faith is always a leap."

"And can you see this old woman leaping?" asked the woman, almost laughing and looking down at her tired body.

"Do not be confused by what you are wearing," said Jacob.

Now the woman was a little confused.

"Our body," said Jacob, "is this moment's costume, and at every moment in our life, there is a costume change."

"But—"

"But our soul," said Jacob, "does not bear the burden of our body."

"So?"

"So," said Jacob, "faith is our soul's leap, not our body's leap."

"Even if you are right, why can't I get my mind around this, Jacob?"

"Because," said Jacob, "what's holding your mind down is your mind!"

THE ABSENT BIRD DOES NOT LEAVE US ABSENT OF ITS SONG.

The old woman looked down from the cliff of losing someone she loved and appeared almost dizzy from the envisioned emotional fall.

Sadness tinged her next question. "When my husband is gone, who will keep me company?"

Jacob's heart ached from this question.

"When we are absent of those we loved," said Jacob, "our faith in knowing we loved and were loved will still keep us company."

"Do you believe this?"

"I used to believe it; now I know it."

"How do you know that?"

"Doctors advise us," said Jacob. "Pain, we listen to. Like you, I have found that pain gets my attention."

When Jacob said this, the woman saw Jacob's own life working its way behind his words.

"Even when we lose the company of people we love," said Jacob, "we are still in their company."

Jacob could feel Ruth take his hand. And he took hers.

Then the woman spoke with a deep sadness in her voice. "Jacob, when my husband is gone, I fear I will feel like a solitary bird on the wire."

"The absent bird," said Jacob, "does not leave us absent of its song."

And when Jacob said this, he said it with more knowing than he wanted to know.

The work in life isn't what you do but who you are.

Jacob now hurried to the school.

The sun was cutting the day at a dramatic angle.

When Jacob arrived, he saw Elizabeth was waiting.

"You seem to have been a big success with the children yesterday," she said. "They think you're a gift."

She said this loud enough for the children to hear, and they gave a shout of approval.

For Jacob, the glee in the children's voices was a like a magic carpet. His spirit felt transported.

Elizabeth motioned with her hand, as if showing someone to their seat, and said, "Jacob, your children."

The questions now came fast and excitedly, and were well beyond the depth of what might have been expected from children.

"Jacob, what does homework have to do with what will be my real work in life?"

"Don't confuse what you want with what you need or what you want to do with what you need to do."

"Huh?"

"The work in life," said Jacob, "isn't what you do but who you are."

"Okay, but why do they call it homework?"

"Because," said Jacob, "the work we don't do will follow us home."

"Jacob," shouted an older boy proudly, "I want to be an inventor."

"Good," said Jacob. "Dare to invent your life; too many people live a life someone else invented for them."

"I think that would make me sad or angry," said the boy.

"Probably both," said Jacob.

"Why?"

"Because when sad goes to sleep, it often wakes up angry."

Another child called out, "Well, I think school is boring."

"Because?" asked Jacob.

"Because there's nothing interesting."

"Nothing is interesting if you are not interested," said Jacob.

"In what?"

"In you."

"You mean I am boring?"

"Not to me," said Jacob.

"So?" asked the boy.

"So…" Jacob's voice lilted into song. "When you're bored and feeling flat, look inside—that's where it's at!"

God is never so with us as when we feel alone.

Now another voice, halting in its admission, said, "Jacob, I'm afraid I'm not meeting my parents' expectations."

"You're not here to meet your parents' expectations."

"I'm not?"

"No," said Jacob, "but you *are* here to meet your own expectations."

"What if my parents are disappointed in me?"

"Good parents also have to parent their expectations."

"So, what's *my* homework?" asked the boy.

"To know what you expect of you."

"What if I expect a lot from myself?"

"Good. Expect more of yourself; accept all of yourself," said Jacob.

Another child now stood up and looked down at the floor even as he raised his voice. "Jacob, sometimes when I go to bed at night, I feel very alone."

"Feeling alone and being alone are not the same," said Jacob.

"So do you say a prayer before you go to bed at night?"

"Yes," said Jacob, "as a reminder."

"And what should we remember?"

"God is never so with us as when we feel alone," said Jacob.

No one has ever found their way who has not felt lost.

For the moment, Jacob and Jacob's children simply sat in the silent reflection of the conversation.

Jacob let the silence sink in. And then…

"Sometimes," said Jacob, "it is when we are around others that we feel most alone."

"My mom says people who talk to themselves are crazy," said a child, almost laughing.

"And my mom," said Jacob, "told me that people who don't talk to themselves are crazy."

"But what do you say, Jacob?"

"I think our mothers should talk to each other, and people should learn each other's names instead of calling them names."

A boy in the back of the room shouted out, "Does it feel different to be alone when you're old?"

"I don't know. I'll let you know when I am old."

The children all laughed and one shouted, "But, Jacob, you must feel old."

"Thank you. I was waiting for that."

"Why?"

"So I could remind you never to confuse how you feel with who you are."

Sophie turned to the others as if she was the teacher and said, "Told you he was smart."

Elizabeth now tentatively raised her hand. "Jacob, can't we argue with our feelings?"

"Oh, we can argue with our feelings," said Jacob. "But feelings aren't built on facts, so arguing with facts won't change how feelings feel."

"Then how can we find our way through our feelings?"

"You have to feel your way," said Jacob.

"To see what feels good?" asked Elizabeth.

"To see if what feels good feels right," said Jacob.

"But what about when something that feels right turns out to be wrong?"

"No one has ever found their way who has not felt lost," said Jacob.

"I heard that you have said that before," said Elizabeth.

"I've been lost before," said Jacob.

An army of sheep led by a lion will defeat an army of lions led by a sheep.

———

Like the fan rotating in the roof of the schoolhouse, Jacob could see that the children's thoughts were also going 'round and 'round.

Then one little girl with hesitant eyes raised her hand.

"Sometimes I get scared in the dark."

"I understand," said Jacob, "but remember this: When you were born, a candle was lit inside you. And it is eternal."

"So I have a light?"

"You are a light!" said Jacob.

"Can I lend my light to others?"

"That's when your light is the brightest."

Another child joined in. "Jacob, I don't think my fears can go to sleep."

"Any of us who think our fears are sleeping are only dreaming," said Jacob.

"Do our fears keep us from being strong?" asked the boy.

"All our strengths," said Jacob, "are born from fears."

"Jacob, that's just a story!" shouted one of the children.

The room was quiet.

"Well then," said Jacob, "maybe this is a good time to tell you a story."

And the children's faces lit up.

"Imagine," said Jacob, "that your life is a wagon, and everything you know about yourself and everything that is yours, is in this wagon.

"Now to pull this wagon, you have been given a team of ten horses. But because all of us have much more fear than faith, let us say that nine of these horses are horses of fear and only one of them is a horse of faith.

"If you put any of the horses of fear at the front of your wagon, they will give you all the excuses you ever give yourself, or others have ever given you, for why you can't do something. And the wagon isn't going anywhere.

"But if you put the one horse of faith at the front of the team, the horses of fear will follow. Your fears will be a source of strength for your faith if you put your faith and not your fears in charge."

The children just sat there quietly, their eyes moving with thought. Then one of the children asked, "Is that a true story?"

"This is what I know to be true. An army of sheep led by a lion will defeat an army of lions lead by a sheep."

"Gosh!" said a boy.

"Can we tell other people this story?" asked a little girl next to Jacob.

And Jacob answered, "Tell your fears that story."

"Jacob," said a boy, slapping his chest and roaring like a lion, "I'm going to tell my sheep that story."

You don't have to die to be reincarnated.

As Jacob headed home, he saw a man standing outside an open window at the school.

"Jacob," said the man, "I wish I'd had a teacher like you when I was in school."

"You're still in school," said Jacob, hurrying along.

"I'm too old to be in school," said the man.

"School's open when we are," said Jacob.

While the man thought about this, the distance between him and Jacob widened.

"So," said the man, now almost shouting, "are you saying the best in me is still being born?"

"Yes," said Jacob. "Happy birthday!"

"But today isn't my birthday."

"Say 'Happy birthday' to anyone who is busy being born," said Jacob.

The man's confusion just increased, so his questions took another turn.

"Jacob does that mean you believe in reincarnation?"

Now Jacob stopped, thought about the question, and answered, "Yes, I believe in reincarnation. I just don't believe you have to die to be reincarnated."

A GREAT FISHERMAN IS SOMEONE WHO
CATCHES HIMSELF JUST IN TIME.

———

As Jacob was walking home, he crossed over a narrow bridge. There, he saw an old man with a rod and reel, and the man shouted at Jacob.

"Hey, mister, do you have anything clever to tell a fisherman?"

"A great fisherman," said Jacob, "is anyone who catches himself just in time."

The man laughed.

"Listen, Jacob, let me be honest. I knew the way you walked home, and I was fishing for you."

"Were you hoping to cook me for dinner?"

The man gave Jacob a slow look up and down. "I don't have a pan that big."

"Desire always has an appetite," said Jacob.

"Is that true even for those who are grateful?" asked the man wryly.

"Even the grateful are not always gratified."

"Well," said the man, "I want you to know I am thankful that a long time ago you taught me, 'Experience is a good teacher, but the tuition is your life.'"

"Either you pay attention," said Jacob, "or you pay later."

"And," said the man, "no matter what we're fishing for in life, it's a good idea to bait our hook with gratitude."

Jacob smiled and said, "So tell me, fisherman, what has fishing taught you about success in life?"

The man returned his smile. "Success can be a lot of fish or the smell of a lot of fish."

Now Jacob laughed loudly. "Please teach me—what else have you learned?"

"I've learned," said the fisherman, "that wisdom was speaking to me when I heard a man named Jacob say, 'Any peace we find in life is its own blessing, and any blessing that does not bring us peace is no blessing.'"

"And now?" asked Jacob.

"And now," said the man, "I have discovered that peace isn't only found by those who are looking for it, but by those who grow weary of overlooking it."

Jacob said nothing for a moment and then asked, "May I make one more inquiry?"

"Of course."

"Have you ever thought of becoming a baker who answers people's questions?"

The people we love and lose are not lost.

With a book in his lap, and the night tapping at his window, Jacob fell asleep.

And while he slept, he dreamed.

In the dream, Jacob's grandfather took Jacob by the hand. "Come, boy, it is time again for us to walk and talk in memory's garden."

And hand in hand they walked.

"Jacob," said his grandfather, "tell me: What did I warn you about the gifts with which you are graced?"

"You said, 'We better like our strengths because we're going to pay for them.'"

"Yes. And when I asked you what you wanted to be when you grew up, what did you say?"

"Awake," said Jacob.

Suddenly the book on Jacob's lap fell to the floor, and Jacob's grip on his grandfather's hand automatically tightened.

"Grandson, are you afraid I am only a dream who will disappear?"

"No, Grandfather," said Jacob, "I know the people we love and lose are not lost."

And Jacob felt his grandfather's hand squeeze back.

Be more. Want less. Care more. Take less.

Jacob's days now had an unexpected ease, which he welcomed.

And the rhythm in this season of Jacob's life was like the repetition in prayer.

This prayer, however, did not rock him to sleep; rather it rocked him awake.

And this was the mind-set that walked with him in harmony with his soul.

"Be more.

"Want less.

"Care more.

"Take less."

Now in the mornings, when Jacob left his home, as it had been at the bakery, there was always someone waiting to see him.

A man who wore his sadness to greet the dawn said to Jacob, "I feel that I have lost my dignity."

"Dignity is not a hat," said Jacob. "Dignity cannot be misplaced unless your mistake was to give it away."

"I understand, but where is my dignity if, for example, someone kicks me?"

"If someone kicks you," said Jacob, "you will be in pain, but you will not have lost your dignity unless you were the one doing the kicking."

"But," asked the man, "if they kick me to the ground, aren't they then the winner, and I am the loser?"

"Dignity is not an outcome," said Jacob. "Dignity can be lost in winning; but even in losing, dignity can be won."

"Are you sure, Jacob?"

"Surely," said Jacob. "It is wise to be cautious of those who confuse kindness with weakness."

INSIDE EVERY PARENT IS A CHILD
NEEDING TO BE LOVED.

———

Elizabeth stood outside the school, wringing her hands and waiting on Jacob's arrival.

Jacob could feel her tension rush to greet him.

"Oh, Jacob, I need to speak with you."

Jacob stood quietly.

"Jacob," said Elizabeth, "Caleb and Sophie's father came to see me. He said you have the children asking questions that make him feel there is a lack of respect."

Jacob said nothing and let the moment find its way.

"He also said," whispered Elizabeth, "that there are two others who are encouraging the community to speak against you."

Again, Jacob showed no concern.

"Aren't you worried?" asked Elizabeth.

"Many years ago," said Jacob, "I heard a wise man say, 'I've had a lot of problems in my life, and most of them never happened.'"

While Jacob and Elizabeth spoke, the children's faces were painted on the windows inside the school.

Clearly, the children were watching the conversation and wondering what was unfolding.

"I just thought you should know and be cautious," said Elizabeth.

"Thank you," said Jacob.

"'Thank you.' That's all you can say?"

"Thank you for caring," said Jacob.

"I care a lot," said Elizabeth.

And Jacob said, "To care much about others, to drink deeply of life, and to hope profoundly for peace—all these are reminders that excess in some things is just right."

"Well, maybe," said Elizabeth, "but perhaps you don't need to be excessively honest when you talk to the children."

"The truth is seldom hidden but often overlooked," said Jacob. "And a half truth is a half lie."

"Okay," said Elizabeth, trying to find her way in this conversation. "But don't you think forthrightness can be too much sometimes?"

"The best defense for the truth," said Jacob, "is the truth."

Elizabeth was feeling frustrated and conflicted. "Oh, Jacob, I just don't know what to do."

"Would you like me to stop coming to the school?"

"No!" said Elizabeth emphatically. "I just wish I could be one of your students and not the teacher."

"There's never been a good teacher who hasn't been a good student," said Jacob.

"Never?"

"Never," said Jacob as he and Elizabeth returned to the classroom.

The children were waiting with their own uncertainty, because they knew something was amiss.

Caleb stood and quieted the others as if he was the teacher and took the floor.

"Jacob, we heard what our father said to our teacher. But we don't know what to say to our parents."

"Tell them you love them," said Jacob.

"Aren't they supposed to tell us that?" asked another girl, laughing.

"Inside every parent," said Jacob, "is a child needing to be loved."

"But aren't they supposed to be the grown-ups?" asked a child in the back of the room.

"There are no grown-ups," said Jacob. "There are only growing-ups."

"What's a growing-up?"

"A growing-up," said Jacob, "is someone who knows we arrive at every moment in life with our bags packed because the moment is leaving."

"And," interjected Sophie, "Jacob says, 'What grows never grows old.'"

Jacob turned his head to her, again wondering how she was so tuned in to his thinking.

"When I grow up, I'm going to be a giant," shouted one of the boys.

"Good," said Jacob. "A giant is anyone who knows we are all sitting on someone else's shoulders."

"Ah, I've heard that before," said the boy.

"The question isn't what you've heard," said Jacob, "but whether you were listening."

"Will that be true even when I get old?" asked the boy.

"Sometimes," said Jacob, "it's the young who have the greatest difficulty listening and the old who have the greatest difficulty hearing."

"Is that a joke?" asked one of the children.

"I can't hear you," said Jacob.

There was a pause, and then all the children laughed.

As did Elizabeth.

And the updraft from the laughter once again lifted even the angels watching over Jacob.

It is the silence between the notes that makes the music.

Jacob wasn't sure if he'd actually decided to do it or it was simply his body's memory willing him, but he took a different path home from the school that day—the one that went past the bakery.

Though the shop was closed, Samuel stood by the ovens dusting and stacking pans so they would be ready for the first bakers when they arrived in the morning.

When a handful of corn meal magically fanned over Samuel's shoulder and onto a pan, Samuel knew who was behind him.

"Oh, Jacob," said Samuel, "I'm very glad you're here."

Samuel's mood was never hidden, and now it was one of concern.

"Jacob, some in the community are confused by your conversations with the children. And the two who misled me and my best intentions when they encouraged you to be the children's teacher now want to silence you."

"It's the silence between the notes that makes the music," said Jacob.

"I tell you about these men plotting against you," said Samuel, "and suddenly I've got a replay of Jacob the Baker giving me wisdom."

"Every silence," said Jacob, "is an original piece of music."

"Oh, I like that," said Samuel, "but listen to me, Jacob. It's the troublemakers I want to silence."

Jacob put his hand on Samuel's shoulder and said, "Anyone…anyone who quiets himself will have more to say."

"I don't think you understand," said Samuel, clearly frustrated. "Jacob, you should be worried."

Jacob, however, appeared to have no interest in entertaining anxiety.

"Not 'should be,' could be," said Jacob. "Of all the things we can choose to be, why choose to be worried?"

"But you're not paying attention," said Samuel.

"Worry is the worst way to pay attention," said Jacob.

"You make it sound like not worrying is heroic," said Samuel.

"You're right," said Jacob. "Sometimes, choosing not to be a worrier is choosing to be a warrior."

"Jacob," said Samuel, "I want to make sure you are clear on what I'm saying. Some of the parents no longer want you to be their children's teacher."

Jacob shrugged his shoulders, suggesting the situation would be solved, but it was not his to solve.

"Tell me, how are you going to manage this?" asked Samuel.

"All of us have influence, but only God holds the reins," said Jacob.

"You think God has a hand even in this?" asked Samuel.

"My friend," said Jacob, "someone who thought he was wise once said to a boy, 'Show me every place that God is, and I will give you a penny.'

"And the boy answered, 'Show me every place God isn't, and I will give you two pennies.'"

Samuel laughed, but his worry was not assuaged.

When Jacob began to speak again, his hands moved as if to pat down the tension. "Samuel, all parents are surprised to discover what they, without intention, have taught their children. And all parents are equally stunned by what their children will one day teach them."

"Maybe," said Samuel, "but children often don't listen to their parents."

"You're right. Children often don't listen to what their parents say, but they do watch what their parents do."

"So?"

"So let us watch."

"Watch what the parents do?"

"And what we do," said Jacob.

"Because now we're older?" asked Samuel.

"Getting older doesn't change who we are," said Jacob, "but it does reveal who we are…even if we're the last to learn it."

Knowing doesn't change the weather.

Jacob lay in the center of his bed.

Sleep was close, but other events were closer.

If you asked Jacob what the consequences might be from the gathering clouds, Jacob would admit, "I don't know."

If pushed on "not knowing," Jacob would answer simply, "Knowing doesn't change the weather."

If you asked him if he was anxious, he would retrieve an oath of awareness from his grandfather.

"If you are depressed, you are living in the past.

"If you are anxious, you are living in the future.

"And if you tell me that it takes courage to live knowing this, you are right.

"Now go and do the work!"

In peace, find gratitude.

The simple, quiet privacies in life gave Jacob access to an inner world no one could take from him and an inner sanctum too many were too willing to give away.

Long ago, Jacob had discovered little could calm large issues like finding peace in a small calm.

And for Jacob, a small calm was not a little thing.

In the morning, it was a taste of the world to come in the heel of rustic bread brushed with soft honey.

On a cold day, it was when he would lay his cheek on the side of the warming oven in the bakery.

On the eve of the seventh day, it was when he leaned into Ruth's memory as she lit candles and wrapped the night's ordained peace around them.

Now Jacob privately ended his day the way it began.

He returned to the spiritual dialectic learned over a lifetime.

In its upward spiraling was his soul's ally.

The words drew him further and further in.

"In gratitude, find prayer.

"In prayer, find faith.

"In faith, find Grace.

"In Grace, find peace.

"In peace, find gratitude."

And in this moment, released from wanting, Jacob found all.

Here was the bouquet of all that is holy.

Here his spirit was intoxicated by the incense of eternity.

> PEOPLE SEEK EMOTIONAL HELP
> WHEN THEY ARE FEELING TOO MUCH
> OR WHEN THEY ARE NOT FEELING AT ALL.

When Jacob woke in the morning, he found he was not alone.

Sitting at the table, in the same chair he sat in as a boy, was Jonah.

Jonah had arrived without announcement, just as he had arrived so many years ago.

This was the boy become a man become a sage, who Jacob, and later Ruth, raised as a son.

The son now looked at his father as if it was simply morning on another day.

Jacob returned the look. But you would be mistaken if you did not note in both of these men the gravity and capacity to look at the common in an uncommon way.

Jonah was an orphan whose grandfather had sent the boy to live and learn with Jacob.

Jonah's grandfather was the Elder of the Council of Sages, as his father had been before him.

And Jacob, who had refused the invitation to serve as the Elder, did accept the role of serving as a teacher for Jonah.

But for Jacob and Jonah, the relationship neither of them expected became more than either could have anticipated.

From its outset, its evolution had been as much about father and son as it had been about mentor and student.

And when the time had come for Jonah to return to his birthplace and assume his role as the Elder of the Council of Sages, the parting between Jacob and Jonah had wrenched at both their hearts.

"It's been a long time," said Jonah.

"Time is born with wings," said Jacob.

"Have you missed me, Father?" asked Jonah from across the table.

"I've missed being called father," said Jacob, smiling.

"I always felt I was your son."

"And when you left," said Jacob, "I felt as if I was losing a son."

"Dear Father," said Jonah, "your love and your wisdom gave me the strength to do the work I was called to do."

Jacob said nothing, then stood and drew Jonah into the circle of his arms. And then he knotted his hands and drew Jonah closer yet.

"I have missed you," said Jonah. "And I heard you may have problems."

Jacob waved away the concern. "No problem goes away until it teaches us what we need to know."

"And people seek emotional help," said Jonah, "when they are feeling too much or when they are not feeling at all."

"And?" asked Jacob.

"And people who think having problems is a problem, have other problems."

"Amen," said Jacob.

"And, Father," said Jonah, taking Jacob by the elbow, "you used to say, 'Life is not a walk in the park, so don't forget to take one.'"

"Yes," said Jacob, taking the hint. "Come, let us walk and talk."

"Like we used to?"

"Like we need to."

"I hear there is worry that what you are teaching the children will challenge their relationships with their parents."

Jacob shrugged. "You know what I say about these things."

"Of course," said Jonah. "I remember. 'First we look up to our parents. Then we look down on them. And then we look at them.'"

"You always were a good student."

"I had a good teacher."

"Parenting," said Jacob, "is a process of moving from manager to consultant, if you're lucky."

"I'm lucky to have you," said Jonah, "and I'm here to help."

And for Jacob, a weight he didn't know he was carrying suddenly got lighter.

Both men smiled.

"I've missed you, Jonah."

"I'm here, Father."

And the father and son, and the son and father, stood next to each other, and saw each other in reflection in time's kindest mirror.

God put one hand in another and felt the hearts fit.

―

Jacob and Jonah took the time to draw current.

They were each equally warmed and renewed by the company, and a shrug of the shoulder or one finger circling in the air was their own language.

Beneath the conversation there was the historic comfort of knowing the unsaid was also shared.

Ruth too joined the conversation, sending her smile to sit between them.

And the radiance of her absent presence was visceral.

When it was time for Jacob to leave for the school, Jonah got up and stood by the door.

"You're joining me?" asked Jacob.

"I am joined to you," said Jonah.

"Of course," said Jacob, nodding at the obvious and patting Jonah's cheek.

The two had not traveled far when they heard a familiar voice coming up behind them.

"What is it with you young men—you don't invite an old friend?"

It was Samuel, and now he wrapped his arms around his friends' shoulders. And two became three became one.

As the men walked, yet again a voice came from behind them.

"Even the learned know it is wise to have strength!"

It was Max, the baker who apprenticed with Jacob and counted himself blessed to have Jacob as a friend.

And it was the same heavily muscled Max on whom Samuel could depend to lift sacks of flour and throw them at the foot of the mixer—as if stacking a ton of grain was Max's poetry.

"Max!" said Jonah, remembering how he used to ride on the giant's shoulders as a boy. "It's been too many years."

The two hugged. And Jacob and Samuel nodded to each other. The phalanx of four became one.

Soon, the school was before them. A cloud of voices floated above it; many of the parents were already at the school, crowding the yard and doorway.

When Jacob, Jonah, Samuel, and Max appeared, their arrival created an undeniable stir among the crowd.

Then, as if by divine intervention, the crowd parted, and Elizabeth, followed by Caleb and Sophie, came from inside the school. They walked through the milling crowd across the yard to where Jacob stood.

Each of the children took one of Jacob's hands, and with him between them, faced the school.

"Jacob," said Elizabeth with a calm in her voice that only exaggerated the brewing discord.

"Elizabeth," said Jacob. "I think you know Samuel and Max. I don't think you've met my son, Jonah."

Elizabeth and Jonah looked at each other. They held that gaze for some time, and then, as if following directions from a cosmic stage director, they both looked down.

And Ruth looked down and smiled.

And the angels looked down and smiled at their work.

And Jacob witnessed Faith.

And God looked down and saw it was good.

And Elizabeth and Jonah stole looks at each other.

And God put one hand in another and felt the hearts fit.

Anyone can count the number
of seeds in an apple.
No one can count the number
of apples in a seed.

Samuel was, of course, the one who took charge, taking the moment to the moment.

With a voice that everyone in the village knew from when their parents first took them to the bakery, Samuel half shouted, "Do we have a problem here, folks?"

Now the crowd was confused. They turned to one another, asking with their eyes if one among them would step forward and say something, anything.

From behind the rows of embarrassed faces, Caleb and Sophie's father and two conspirators pushed forward.

"Our friend," said one of the men, barely masking his anger and pointing to the children's father, "feels that Jacob is teaching the children ideas that challenge him as a parent."

Samuel looked at the two conspirators, his eyes hardening with an unsympathetic determination seldom witnessed by any in the community.

And when Samuel spoke again, his voice was like a searing shank of tempered metal pulled from the blacksmith's fire.

"Are you two friends of the father or an enemy of Jacob? Which is it? Who are these snakes selling us an apple?"

The men withered under this question, embarrassed for themselves, and shrank back into the crowd.

The children's father still stepped forward, though, even as he moved away with distaste from the retreating men. It was clear, however, that words failed him, and vulnerability was steering him.

Their father's pain was in turn painted on the faces of Caleb and Sophie. They looked at Jacob for direction, and Jacob nodded, urging them in the direction of their father.

The children walked toward their father, each in turn taking one of his hands, and brought him across the open area to where Jacob was standing.

"No matter what our work is in life," said Jacob, "dignity doesn't come with the job. Dignity is what we bring to the job."

"And," said Sophie, "Jacob says, 'We all have different jobs, but all work is sacred.'"

Their father listened, even as his eyes were fixed on his children.

"All of our relationships in life," said Jacob, "are reciprocal trade agreements. I give you this; you give me that. But this is not true for parents and teachers.

"Parents and teachers have a higher agreement. Parents and teachers give, and what they get is the giving."

Jacob put his hand on the man's shoulder and said, "Do not kiss your children so they will kiss you back. Kiss them so they will kiss their children and their children's children."

On hearing this, Jonah and Elizabeth as one looked to the father and then to each other.

Sophie prodded Jacob. "Tell him about the apple. He'll understand that."

"Yes, Sophie," said Jacob, looking at her father with caring, not accusation.

"Scripture tells us a good child is the apple of a parent's eye," said Jacob. "And anyone can see that in your eyes…But while anyone can count the number of seeds in an apple, no one can count the number of apples in a seed."

"We are the seeds in your apple, Daddy," said Sophie.

"And in your children, and your children's children, are your orchards across time," said Jacob.

"We love you, Daddy," said Sophie, "and if we gave you disrespect…"

"Then we have disrespected ourselves," said Caleb, finishing his sister's sentence. "Jacob also taught us that."

And the father bent down, and on his knees drew his children into his embrace.

And in this sacred moment, Jacob heard the sacred teaching: "God is present whenever a peace treaty is signed."

People of all faiths are of one faith if their religion is kindness.

―――

"Well, then," said Max as he stepped forward and slapped his hands together. "I think we have that wrapped up. Any other complaints?"

The crowd in front of the school churned a moment. Feet shuffled as the parents tried to find their way with what would or should happen next.

A middle-aged woman walked to the front of the crowd. "Jacob, we don't know if you know how challenging it is to be a parent."

Before Jacob could reply, Jonah came forward to meet the woman.

Jonah spoke slowly and with deep compassion. "Jacob is my father. When I became an orphan…"

But before Jonah could say any more, people began whispering to one another, pulling at their neighbor's attention, each beckoning the other in awe of who was speaking.

"That's Jonah. He's the Elder of the Council of Sages."

"He's a saint."

"I didn't know he was Jacob's son."

"When I became an orphan," said Jonah, beginning again, "Jacob opened his home and heart. And he raised me to be a man."

"And he wasn't always so easy to raise," said Max, reminding everyone that even saints were once children.

Then another man came out of the crowd. "Jonah, we all hold you in the highest regard, and Jacob too, but sometimes being a parent is confusing. Can you tell us something you remember Jacob teaching you?"

Jonah looked into the man's eyes, and in a voice that was eerily like Jacob's said, "Jacob taught me to believe in myself and to believe in more than myself. He taught me that to take God's hand, we have to offer someone else a hand. And he taught me that things don't have to be good for us to be great."

Murmurs of approval rippled through the crowd.

"And if any of you have heard any of this before," said Jonah, "remember, the only question the truth asks is, 'Are you listening now?'"

There were more murmurs, and now, some smiles.

"All right," said Samuel, resting his hand on Jacob's shoulder, "let us not be confused any longer. All of us have learned something from this man even as he would declare that we have been *his* teacher.

"All of you know where Jacob lives. And if you have forgotten, let me remind you. Jacob lives at the corner of hope, wisdom, and faith. And all of you have visited him there.

"He has come into all of our lives with unarmed truth and unconditional love, and that is his triumph not over us but for us.

"The truth is that all of us, young and old, are Jacob's children. And as Jacob would remind us, even when school is out, school is in.

"So, now, I will be the teacher and ask any of you, tell me something you learned about life from Jacob the Baker."

For a moment, nothing happened, and then a man with broad shoulders stepped forward. "I am a farmer, and Jacob taught me that if you pray to grow or grow anything in life, you have to plant hope to reap faith."

From the back of the crowd, someone shouted, "Jacob taught me that when we lose hope, we lose our way."

"When we were children," said a mother holding her child, "our parents would tell us stories to put us to sleep. Jacob told us stories to wake us up."

An older woman stepped up, took off the scarf covering her head, and with an air of beatitude said, "Jacob taught me that if you think your life is blessed then the best way to say thank you is to be a blessing to others."

A little girl with a huge grin drew her foot in the sand and said, "Jacob taught me that God smiles on those who smile back."

An old man leaned on his cane and with tears in his eyes said, "I have seen too much pain in my life between people who call themselves people of faith. Jacob taught me that people of all faiths are of one faith if their religion is kindness."

Elizabeth stepped past her fears, looked at the others, looked at Jacob, and then locked her gaze on Jonah. "Jacob taught me that feelings are the facts of life. And not to let the past kidnap my future."

Jonah returned Elizabeth's focus with his own and witnessed with an unanticipated passion what he had prayed for, and waited for, and for what was now looking back at him.

And while all the things that were being said were said, Jacob held his own counsel, in his own prayer, in a world of gratitude where words failed.

Then Jacob, from within Jacob, surprising all, called out the two men who had plotted against him.

The two came forth sheepishly. And Jacob said, "When Jacob's son Joseph again met the brothers who threw him in a pit and sold him into slavery, the brothers feared for their lives.

"But they were reminded, 'Though you meant it for evil, God meant if for good.'"

"So what will become of us?" asked the two, fearful the crowd might now turn on them.

"Life isn't only what we can give each other but what we can forgive in each other," said Jacob. "So you will be what you have always been: my brothers."

And Jacob embraced the two men. And they wept in the arms of acceptance.

And Jacob felt an invisible Hand lift his gaze upward and draw back the veil on Grace.

And the town, and the school, and all standing on God's green earth found themselves now under an achingly beautiful rainbow.

And the radiating transformation experienced by all and from all rose up as a single voice in prayer.

And to this day, all in attendance still swear they heard "Amen" in a thunderclap of affirmation.

WE'RE NOT EXPECTED TO FINISH OUR WORK,
BUT NEITHER ARE WE EXCUSED FROM IT.

―――

Jacob and Samuel sat on the porch outside Jacob's home.
Each of them was replaying the day in their mind's eye.
And as usual, each of them could sense what the other was thinking—and when it was the allotted moment to open the silence to a shared conversation.
"Well," said Samuel, as if testing the water.
"Yes," said Jacob.
"Yes, it was," said Samuel.
"I'm not sure how much more needs to be said," said Jacob.
"Nope," said Samuel. "And besides, many years ago you said, 'Anything said about the truth is a lie.'"
"The word 'tree' never grows apples," said Jacob.
"We are growing older," said Samuel, pulling at a gray hair.
"But what grows never grows old," said Jacob, even as he pulled at a gray hair on his own head.
"You see how you do that? You always turn things inside out."
"Friendship turns us inside out," said Jacob.
"And Jacob's gift is Jacob," said Samuel.
Jacob weighed this. And weighed it again.
"Well, okay," said Samuel, "aren't you the baker who said: 'There is love and work in life. If we're fortunate, we love our work; if we're wise, we'll work at love'?"

Jacob smiled.

"And aren't you the man who reminds us we're not expected to finish our work, but neither are we excused from it?"

"Yes," said Jacob softly.

"And aren't you the man who says, 'If you book a seat on the excuse train, you'll miss the train that's leaving'?"

"Yes," said Jacob more softly yet.

"So keep working, Jacob the Baker," said Samuel. "We're all counting on you…You *knead* us, and we need you."

And Samuel laughed at his wit.

And Jacob just smiled.

And the friends sat under the stars.

And the conversation continued.

Forever may not be long enough.

―――

When Jacob and Samuel went outside to talk after dinner, Jonah offered to walk Elizabeth home.

While Jacob and Samuel shared the stars above them, for Jonah and Elizabeth, the moon was theirs alone.

"May I ask you a question?" said Elizabeth.

"Sure."

"I know now you are the Elder of the Council of Sages, but aren't you pretty young to be the Elder?"

Jonah laughed and then said, "A long time ago, my father taught me: 'There is old wine in young barrels and young wine in old barrels.'"

"Oh," said Elizabeth, with both amusement and respect in her voice.

Jonah could read the look in her eyes and took value in it.

"Thank you," he said, wanting to say more and meaning even more.

Elizabeth answered with her glance and let it linger.

Jonah held her look.

As the path narrowed, their shoulders brushed.

"I'm sorry," said Jonah.

"I'm not," said Elizabeth. Jonah the Elder, was young at this, she realized. She asked, "Are you going to stay with Jacob for a while?"

"I wasn't planning to, but…"

"I would like you to," said Elizabeth.

"I think you should," said Ruth in a voice that spoke as a breeze.

"I think I should," said Jonah, and felt the breeze brush his cheek.

"Perhaps we will become good friends," said Elizabeth.

"Perhaps has no end," said Jonah.
"Well then, perhaps forever," said Elizabeth, putting faith over fear.
"Well then," said Jonah, "forever may not be long enough."

About the Author

Noah benShea is one of North America's most respected and beloved poet-philosophers. He is a Pulitzer Prize–nominated, internationally best-selling author of twenty-seven books that have been translated into eighteen languages, including the Jacob the Baker series. He is a scholar and theologian who has spoken at numerous prestigious universities and institutions, including the Library of Congress and the U.S. Department of Defense, and he has been published by Oxford University Press and The World Bible Society in Jerusalem.

He was a dean at UCLA at the age of twenty-two, and by age thirty, he was a Fellow at several esteemed think tanks. He has served as a private adviser to corporate and political leaders and occupied such posts as Visiting Professor of Philosophy at the University of California SF Medical School; Philosopher in Residence at the Department of Internal Medicine at Cottage Health Hospitals, Santa Barbara; and Ethicist for the Sansum Diabetes Research Institute. He was nominated for the Grawemeyer Award for Ideas that Improve the World Order, was the National Laureate for the ALS Association. and National Philosopher for Foundations Recovery Network.

Noah is the founder and executive director of The Justice Project. Born in Toronto, he is a long-term resident of Santa Barbara, California, and lives part of each year in Italy.

To learn more, visit: www.NoahbenShea.com.

Contact Noah at: Noah@NoahbenShea.com.

CPSIA information can be obtained
at www.ICGtesting.com
Printed in the USA
FSHW01n0758230918
52480FS